ALSO BY GARRETT HONGO

POETRY

The River of Heaven

Yellow Light

NONFICTION

Volcano: A Memoir of Hawai`i

CORAL ROAD

CORAL ROAD

Poems

Garrett Hongo

ALFRED A. KNOPF   NEW YORK   2011

THIS IS A BORZOI BOOK
PUBLISHED BY ALFRED A. KNOPF

www.aaknopf.com/poetry

Knopf, Borzoi Books, and the colophon are registered
trademarks of Random House, Inc.

"The Wartime Letters of Hideo Kubota" art is courtesy of the family of Tamaichi,
Shizuyo, and Katsuichi Tanaka; the "Art of Fresco" artwork is courtesy of the U.S.
Army, USAG Livorno, Camp Darby; all other art is from the poet's collection.

Library of Congress Cataloging-in-Publication Data
Hongo, Garrett Kaoru, [date]
Coral road : poems / by Garrett Hongo.—1st ed.
p. cm.
"This is a Borzoi Book."
ISBN 978-0-307-59476-1
I. Title.
PS3558.O48C67 2011
811'.54—dc22
2011011560

Front-of-jacket photograph: Japanese cemetery,
Kahuku, Hawai`i, July 2004. Courtesy of the author
Jacket design by Chip Kidd

Manufactured in the United States of America
First Edition

for Hideo and Tsuruko Kubota, I.M.

A spreading oak, that near a linden grows . . .

Hone `ana i ka mana`o
E naue ku`u kino
—Queen Kapi`olani, "Ipo Lei Manu"

Kane wa kachiken
Wash'ya horehore yo
Ase to namida no
Tomo kasegi

—Anon., "Hole Hole Bushi,"
Japanese cane worker's song, 19th century

This, alas,
Was but a dream: the times had scattered all
These lighter graces, and the rural ways
And manners which it was my chance to see
In childhood were severe and unadorned,
The unluxuriant produce of a life
Intent on little but substantial needs,
Yet beautiful—and beauty that was felt.

—William Wordsworth, *The Prelude*, 1805

Contents

THIS SHEET IS FOR STEERAGE PASSENGERS.

Required by the regulations of the Secretary of Commerce and Labor of the United States, under Act of Congress approved February 20, 1907, to be delivered to the United States Immigration Officer by the Commanding Officer of any vessel having such passengers on board upon arrival at a port in the United States.

S.S. *Nippon Maru* sailing from *Nagasaki, Japan* *July* 1907   Arriving at Port of *Honolulu* 190

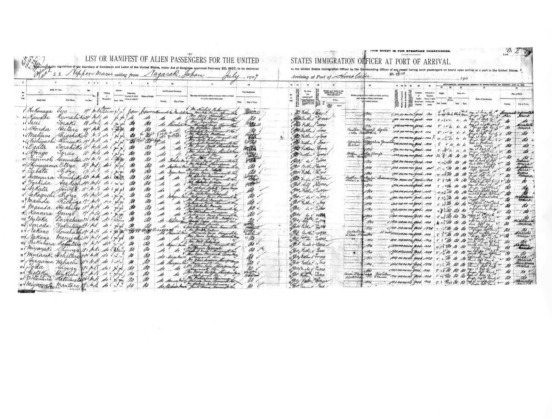

PROLOGUE

An Oral History of Blind-Boy Liliko`i

I came out of Hilo, on the island of Hawai`i,
lap-steel and Dobro like outriggers on either side of me,
shamisen strapped to my back as I went up the gangplank
to the *City of Tokio* running inter-island
to Honolulu and the big, pink hotel on Waikīkī
where all the work was back in those days.
I bought a white linen suit on Hotel Street
as soon as I landed, bought a white Panama too,
and put the Jack of Diamonds in my hatband for luck.
Of my own, I had only one song, "Hilo March,"
and I played it everywhere, to anyone who would listen,
walking all the way from the Aloha Tower to Waikīkī,
wearing out my old sandals along the way.
But that's okay. I got to the Banyan Tree
on Kalakaua and played for the tourists there.
The bartenders didn't kick me out or ask for much back.
Zatoh-no-bozu, nah! I went put on the dark glasses and pretend I blind.
I played the slack-key, some hulas, an island rag,
and made the tourists laugh singing *hapa-haole* songs,
half English, half Hawaiian. Come sundown, though,
I had to shoo—the contract entertainers would be along,
and they didn't want *manini* like me
stealing the tips, cockroach the attention.
I'd ride the trolley back to Hotel Street
and Chinatown then, change in my pocket,
find a dive on Mauna Kea and play *chang-a-lang*
with the Portagee, *paniolo* music with Hawaiians,
slack-key with anybody, singing harmonies,
waiting for my chance to bring out the *shamisen*.
But there hardly ever was. Japanee people
no come the bars and brothels like before.
After a while, I give up and just play whatever,

dueling with `ukulele players for fun,
trading licks, make ass, practicing that
happy-go-lucky all the tourists seem to love.
But smiling no good for me. I like the stone-face,
the no-emotion-go-show on the face,
all feeling in my singing and playing instead.
That's why Japanee style suits me best.
Shigin and *gunka,* ballads about warriors
and soldier song in Japanee speech.
I like the key. I like the slap and *chi-to-shan* of *shamisen.*
I feel like I galvanize
and the rain go drum on me,
make the steel go ring inside.
Ass when I feel, you know, ass when I right.
Ass why me, I like the blues. Hear 'em first time
from one *kurombo* seaman from New Orleans.
He come off his ship from Hilo Bay, walking downtown
in front the S. Hata General Store
on his way to Manono Street looking for
one crap game or play cards or something.
I sitting barber shop, doing nothing but reading book.
He singing, yeah? sounding good but sad.
And den he bring his funny guitar from case,
all shining metal with *puka* holes
like one pointsettia spidering over the box.
Make the tin-kine sound, good for vibrate.
Make da kine shake innah bones sound
like one engine innah blood. Penetrate.
He teach me all kine songs. Field hollers, he say,
da kine slave g'on use for call each oddah
from field to field. Ju'like cane workers.
And rags and marches and blues all make up
from diss black buggah from Yazoo City,
up-river and a ways, the blues man say.
Spooky. No can forget. Ass how I learn for sing.

LIST OR MANIFEST OF ALIEN IMMIGRANTS FOR THE COMMISSIONER OF IMMIGRATION.

Required by the regulations of the Secretary of the Treasury of the United States, under Act of Congress approved March 3, 1893, to be delivered to the Commissioner of Immigration by the Commanding Officer of any vessel having such passengers on board, upon arrival at a port in the United States.

S.S. _Peru_, sailing from _Yokohama, Dec. 2 1902_, arriving at port of _Honolulu, Dec 12 1902_

NAME IN FULL	Age	Sex	Married	Calling or Occupation	Nationality	Last residence	Final destination			Age										
Soraichi Yamamoto	40		yes	farmer	yes	Japanese	Hiroshima	Honolulu	yes	self	$52.00 shore	no		no		no	no	no	Good	no
Masanichi Sueda	22										48									
Senuikichi Sanjo	20										46									
Shimutaro Okahira	30										55									
" Yuayoshi	36		wife	NO					husband	45										
Kajo Hirahara	24		farmer	yes					self	52										
Shigoro Miyuta	42		no	NO						49										
Matsutaro Suga	29		yes							55										
Jirobei Nakatsuka	19		no	yes		Yamaguchi				55										
Saburogumo Hiroshi	20									48										
Yoshikichi Kuroshige	19			NO						46										
Shinsuke Nagaoka	20			yes						46										
Toyoshino Araki	21		yes			Hiroshima	Ve. App RP 4-9-35 CF P 706			46										
Chosaku Koga	22		yes	NO		Fukuoka				45										
" Harvys	19		wife						husband	49										
Hisauké Kikutake	24		farmer						self	52										
" Asae	18		wife						husband	45										
Yoshikichi Gayama	24		farmer						self	56										
" Wasa	24		wife						husband	45										
Katsutaro Hagiwara	20		farmer	yes					self	47										
" Survys	25		wife	NO					husband	48										
Joishi Katsuoka	27		farmer						self	47										
" Musashy	21		wife						husband	45										
Kichi Oekajima	24		farmer	yes	App R.P. Oec. 4-11-53 CF P 741				self	57										
" Othrina	9		wife	NO	App R.P. Jan 4-11-37 CF P 842				husband	50										
Hikichi Ezaki	19		farmer						self	50										
" Orkuno	16		wife						husband	45										
Jaddichi Nakahara	24		farmer	yes		Hiroshima			self	67	2d time									
" Yoshii	9		wife			"			husband	45	1st time									
" Sadato	1		no	child		"														

Ex. Dec. 15/02 at Quarantine Sta.

All Katsuma

V Sis. Lt Nos 1-3-5-16 + 14

I

CORAL ROAD

The Festival of San Giovanni

Orange ghosts of torchlight washing over the innocent faces around me,
And it's like we're children again—three doctors, a philosopher, my wife, and I—
Trekked down from the Austrian villa up the promontory to a Lombardian village
And its festival shore of Lago di Como on the dockside steps
of the Grand Hotel Serbelloni.

Shelly and McGrath lead our group's processional, hoisting their stalks of flames,
Gathering us under their sponsoring globes of light, while we follow down the
curve of asphalt drive
To a lakeside walkway, the cool dusk descending in a choir
Of slate cloud-cover, a light chop-kicking up,
Fishermen on the shoreline dipping their poles, the crowd around us
murmurous with glee.

In Hawai`i, along the North Shore,
We who remember sometimes make another pilgrimage, from Waialua to Hale`iwa,
Then along the old railway route past Waimea and the Sts. Peter and Paul Catholic Church,
Its lookout Jesus on the topmost bend in the road, garlanded with leis from passersby,
To Pupukea and below the bluffs past Pipeline to Sunset Beach and the beginning
of the Castle & Cooke sugar lands,
Cane fields abandoned now, unruly museum of gigantic grasses,
green and tasseled elegies of loss.

The path we take winds along Bellagio's lakefront, past the ferry terminals
and old promenade,
Under the gingko trees by the ruined boathouse and little strip of park
Where they have the monthly flea market, then up the road past the Villa Melzi
and its kept gardens
That Byron and Shelley once admired, that Liszt and his lover used for rendezvous.
There are deep, green lawns,
Monumental shadows swimming along the ground and up the walls of each villa we pass,

Drifts of conversation like blossom-filled boats scenting the air

                               with cloudbursts of Spanish,

Moondrifts of English and Italian.

In 1919, twenty Japanese laborers once fled their contracts, the first in the islands

                                      who dared strike—

For better pay, write historians, but, to me and this murk of night, it was

                                       for the story of it.

I think of them, wrapped in wind, as I am tonight, bowl of the Pacific at their

                                left shoulders as they fled,

Shallop of freedom on the horizon beyond where they could see, its fisherman

                                   pulling his line,

Checking his traps, slowly raveling up his string of baited baskets

Behind the shimmering wake of his drifting boat, bark of promise

                                visible to none but the settling dark.

Coral Road

I keep wanting to go back, across an ocean, blue-gray and uncaring,
White cowlicks of waves at the continental shore, then the midsea combers
Like white centipedes far below the jetliner that takes me there.
And across time too, to 1920 and my ancestors fleeing Waialua Plantation,
Trekking across the northern coast of O`ahu, that whole family
                              of first Shigemitsu
Walking in *geta* and sandals along railroad ties and old roads at night,
Sleeping in the bushes by day, *ha`alelehana*—runaways
From the labor contract with Baldwin or American Factors.

My grandmother, ten at the time, hauling an infant brother on her back,
Said there was a white coral road in those days, pieces of crushed reef
Poured like gravel over the brown dirt, and, at night, with the moon up,
As it was those nights during their flight, silver shadows on the sea,
It lit their path like a roadway made of dust from the Ocean of Clouds.
Tsuki-no-michi is what they called it, the Moon Road from Waialua to Kahuku.

There is little to tell and few enough to tell it to—
A small circle of relatives gathered for reunion
At some beach barbecue or Elks Club veranda in Waikīkī,
All of us having survived that plantation sullenness
And two generations of labor in the sugar fields,
Having shed most all memory of travail and the shame of upbringing
In the clapboard shotguns of ancestral poverty.

                              Who else would even listen?
Where is the Virgil who might lead me through the shallow underworld of this history?
And what demiurge can I say called to them, loveless ones,
        through twelve-score stands of cane
Chittering like small birds, nocturnal harpies in the feral constancies of wind?

*

All is diffuse, like knowledge at dusk, a veiled shimmer in the sea

As schools of baitfish boil and revolve in their iridescent globes,

Turning to the olive dark and the drop-off back to depth below,

Where they shiver like silver penitents—a cloud of thin, summer moths—

While rains chill the air and pockmark the surface of the sands at Sans Souci,

And we scatter back inside to a humble Chinese buffet and cool *sushi*

Spread on Melamine platters on a starched white ribbon of shining cloth.

Waimea-of-the-Dead

Waimea, a village on Kaua`i's southwest shore, is where they went first—
Thatched huts and mud floors, sewers for streets, or pathways, really,
Like sluices in heavy rains—human mire, cane bagasse, and runoff around their feet.

I went there once, but it was summer, and I was with my sons, our first gentle ones.
They were teen and preteen then, soft and bewildered by everything—
The turquoise Gatorade half-bowl of Hanalei Bay, calm as bathwater,
Lo`ikalo taro fields, brown terraces of tremulous green hearts
                                        lolling in the light afternoon wind,
and the viridian elephant's feet of mountains rising into lavish clouds
                                        purple as *poi.*
We hiked the swampy Alaka`i one day and saw birds big as crows,
Yet plumed like parakeets, fiery orange and yellow, and stared
At the ribboned varicolors of rocky chasms and felt the wind lift us from our collars
                                        flapping like loose sails.

One night, the clearest evening of the year, I took them to Bon Odori,
Where the living dance for the expiation of the dead caught in limbo
To release them from trial and permit a passage to *nirvana*—an ultimate heaven.
Counterclockwise in summer robes, holding fans, twirling loose, draping sleeves,
The dancers would circle around the *yagura,* a tower in the middle of a ball field,
And laughter would rise like sugary smoke from the broiling fires at every booth,
While folks clapped hands to *ondo* rhythms, pre-millennium country tunes
About the rice harvest, mining coal, or simply lovelorn travail.
I always liked the clarinets and saxophones, honking softly like pelicans at the shore—
Their old, pentatonic melodies and lugubrious trills, cornier-than-thou.

But my sons grew up with none of these, far from this past that was, to me,
The *real* world and its genuine glory—not the strained exile I suffered
Pushing a grocery cart up the cereal aisles of a sad Safeway.

*

This was home to me—
Wandering a sandy parade ground while the PA blared with *min'yō* and lantern lights
Bobbed like glass floats along the intricate nets of electrical wire strung above us,
The barker's call of the next tune and his welcome of a dance club from Maui,
Men in their seventies, fit and muscled, with white-haired crew cuts and creviced faces,
Women in ricebag aprons and embroidered shawls, *geta* clapping their heels
                                        as they walked
from pool to luminous pool of neighbors and friends, the pre-school children
crouching arrhythmically inside the dance-ring and stamping their feet
        just behind the beat.

We flowed along, anonymous to all, gathering brief, impolite stares,
For, although we might look as if we belonged, no one knew us,
Or even the favor of our faces, as none shared our blood, and we were strangers
                                        to this edge of Paradise,
Ourselves ghosts of our ancestors among the living of Waimea,
Who could barely see us, squinting, rubbing their eyes, and blinking,
Trying to bring our bodies into focus, our faces like shadows in a mirror,
Silhouettes of darkened lanterns not quite lit by the glow from another close by.

I thought to make a prayer then, and we took a few steps away from the dancing
Towards the long, flower-lined entry path to the shrine and offertory,
Decorative, straw-wrapped tubs of *shōyu* stacked in pyramids along
                                        each side of the *butsuma.*
I showed the boys the slow way to approach, heads bowed, hands in *gasshō,*
As I myself learned at the monastery, the priest taking my hands and lifting
                                        my thumbs,
Taking my head firmly and inclining it down like a barber would a boy's.
And then the three-point genuflection—knees on the floor, forehead touching
                                        the carpet,

Hands upraised over the ears as if they were flowers floating on the surface

of a pool

Where you'd just dipped your face to search its bottom for roots.

Namu Amida Butsu we murmured, *Homage to the World-Compassionate One,*
And a winding veil of *emptiness* spun alert inside my heart, stranger in these shadows,
My soul aswerve like a battered moth, misdirected in summer flight
        by the gentle web of pitching festival lights.

Pupukea Shell

I think of the old Pupukea Shell station on Kamehameha Highway—
Two pumps, '60s glass-and-concrete architecture, a roll-up, two-car garage front,
Mortise-and-tenon awning, and the great, yellow *Pecten langfordi,*
Short collar under the fanlike ribs, floating like a child's painting
     of a sunrise
Above the straightaway seafloor of asphalt road just past Chun's Reef
     along the North Shore.

It never meant the corporate name to me, but rather the moon in summer seasons,
Its only competitor for luminescence nights we drove the highway back
                from Honolulu,
And those nights on the Fourth when cousins would hand me sparklers already lit,
Then a huge toad, dry and cold in my hands and on my shoulders,
Then an amber strip of dried and sweetened cuttlefish, chewy and aromatic.

It was owned by relatives—the Yoshikawas, sturdy Moloka`i people married
               into us Shigemitsus,
who hosted the summer gatherings of the matriarchal clan at their gas station
           and grounds—
out back a Meiji-style peaked and fluted roof house,
     splendid lawns, plumeria trees, and *tī* plants at the property lines.
This is near Shark's Cove where all the tourists and some locals snorkel now,
Diving for bubbly glimpses of blue fantailed fish,
     schools of yellow tangs, and the rotor-finned *humuhumu.*
When I see it these days, boarded up and rusting,
     the window glass of the office spiderwebbed with cracks,
The pumps gone like pulled teeth and the timbers and underside of the awning
Blackened with mildew and spotted with blooms of a brown, fungal scourge,
I remember that a pair of lovers met there once—a shopgirl and a dark local boy
     with long, black surfer's hair reddened by the sun.
He wore jeans and a brown shirt that said "Cecilio" across his breast,
Had the thick, calloused hands of a laborer, but eyes that shone like light
Striking the sandy bottom of the sea in the soft waters of the lagoon just offshore.

*

He wrote in a small copybook every day,

                scribblings and verses on his lunch break,

His bare feet wicking in and out of the blue rubber sandals he wore

                    as he bent over the pages.

He'd take the night shift, summer or winter, keep the lights on and pumps going

For all the locals and tourists till past midnight, frogs singing, the air cool as thought.

It was the only station open past six on the whole North Shore,

So it got the business of commuters to town and all the straggler tourists

                headed late back to Waikīkī.

Cecilio liked the inconstant flow, the chance to meditate between customers

As he scanned lamplit eyes over the pink lagoon at sunset, imagining *whatevah*

      in the silence of cormorants,

Black pens dipping their yellow beaks into the magentaed seas.

Once, just before closing, when Cecilio was at his desk bending over Creole pentameters,

A wanderer came by on foot, tapping at the glass of the office, making him glance

Away from his strange, literate work.

      "I saw a light," she said, uncovering her hair,

Which she had shielded beneath silver-gray silk. "And I've lost my way.

Can I rest here a while?"

But from where did she come? this *haole fanciulla* dressed in thin, black clothes,

A shawl like a Portuguese grandmother's,

Chinese dancing shoes made for acrobats buckled at the back,

Skin like goat's milk fresh in the pail, and black, black curly hair?

She was a vision like the Mary who gave the Virgin Birth

He knew from Catholic school, and like the stories people told of Pele,

The goddess testing the mortal by taking human form.

                    *

But she suppose' to be ol' . . .

Cecilio said within, rising from his battered chair, its wooden legs scraping

the concrete floor,

His breath growing shallower to witness beauty immaculate amidst the mundane.

"My name is Lucia," she said. "I paint island flowers on beach glass . . .

I embroider orchid boats on linen seas . . ."

And the midnight half-moon

Rose like a spreading, silver fan floating on the ink-dark ocean of the sky.

Cane Fire

At the bend of the highway just past the beachside melon and papaya stands,
Past the gated entrance to the Kuilima Hotel on the point where Kubota once
                                        loved to fish,
The cane fields suddenly begin—a soft green ocean of tall grasses
And waves of wind rolling through them all the way to the Ko`olau,
        a velvet green curtain of basalt cliffs covered in mosses.
Tanaka Store comes up then, *makai* side of the highway, *towards the sea,*
And, whatever it looks like now—curio conchs dangling from its porch rafters
Festooned with birdcages of painted bamboo, wooden wafers of old shave-ice
                                        cones and prices—
I think of stories and photos from nearly a century ago
When Gang no. 7 worked hoe-*hana* and *happai-ko* out near here,
Bending to weed the hoe rows or shouldering a thirty-pound bundle of sticky cane,
Trying not to think of the fresh tubs of cold *tōfu* lying on the wet plank floors
                                        in its grocery aisles
Or the money they owed for bags of rice, cans of Crisco, and *moxa* pellets
They used for flaming the skin on their backs at night, relieving aches with
                                        flashes of pain,
Remembering fire was for loneliness, smoke was for sorrow.

And, if I see a puffer fish, dried and lacquered, full of spikes and pride,
Suspended over a wood-frame doorway as I glance back while driving by,
Or if the tall television actor with long blond hair and a cowboy's gait
Walks from the parking lot towards the picnic tables of the decrepit shrimp shack
Where the old icehouse used to be, where the cameras and film crew now stand,
I'm not going to lean forward into wanting or desire, amusements of my time,
But remember instead that Pine Boy died here one afternoon in 1925.

I know this because I count from the year my grandmother was born in 1910,
The year Twain died and the comet passed close to them sitting among the cane at night,
A pearly fireball and long trail of alabaster light over the empty Hawaiian sea,
And forward to the story of how she was fifteen when the *lunas* called her to calm him.

*

Matsuo was her adopted brother, a foundling of Hawaiian blood raised Shigemitsu
And sent, at sixteen, to work the cane fields with his brothers and uncles.
No incidents until the day the field bosses ordered cane fires to be lit,
Workers oiling the roots and grass, torchers coming through to light the cane,
Burn its leaves down to harvestable stalks that could be cut and stacked.

Something flamed in Matsuo too, because he grabbed a *luna* and cut his throat,
Ran into the blazing fields, and could be heard whimpering *ju'like one pig,*
His cries coming through the rising smoke and crackle of the cane fires.

What words he said I've never been told—only that he moved within the fields,
Staying ahead or within the fire, and could not be coaxed out
                                        or pursued with dogs or on a horse.

Among the Gang, there was no one who doubted his own death
                                        should they follow him.
But Tsuruko, his sister, was called, *tita* who had nursed with him,
Rushed out of school and brought in the manager's car out to the fields,
The man opening the door and taking her hand *as if she haole wahine ladat!*
As she stepped from the cab and onto the scorched plantation earth.

The image I have is of her walking over opened ground absolutely cleared of cane,
The brown and black earth mounded up around her as she stood among small hillocks
                                        as if a score of graves had just been dug,
The soft, inconstant breezes pressing a thin cotton dress against her skin,
Her back to the crowd while she says something into the wind that only the cane
                                        and Matsuo could hear.

And then his crying ceased and he emerged magically from a curtain of smoke and cane,
His eyes tarred and patched with burnt oil and charcoaled with molasses.
He stood out for an instant, in front of wicking flames,
Then felt the bead of a rifle on him, and he slipped quickly back in,
The cane fires muffling whatever words he might have called as they took him.

*

The crouching lion of a lava bluff juts near the road,

And I know the jeep trail will come up next,

A cattle fence and white and brown military sign its marker.

It's where the radar station is, far past the fields and up-mountain

Where the sluice waters start and the apples blossom,

Leaving white popcorn flowers dappling the mud with faint,

                    perishable relicts of rage and beauty.

A Child's Ark

Hot Los Angeles summer days, late '50s, a seven-year-old
Shut in the tiny midtown apartment on South Kingsley Drive,
I'd flip on the TV to the black-and-white game shows,
Rerun comedies and half-hour detective dramas,
Seeking company, avoiding the soaps, news, and cartoons.

One of my favorites for a while was a show called *Kideo Village,*
In which kids would wend their way through the attractive curves
Of a game path spooling through the sound studio and its faux lampposts,
Small minimalist archways, doors, pushcarts, and street stands
Set up and interspersed along the telegenic route—
A bakery, a toyshop, the ice cream parlor, etc.
The tragedies strewn in the way would be a bookstore or piggy bank—
For one you'd have to lose a turn and stay inside to read a book,
For the other, you'd give up spending for a certificate of virtue.

The glory was a pet store of fluffy animals—
Nose-twitching rabbits bearing sachets of cash around their necks,
A dog hitched to a wagon filled with sacks of stage gold.
Wealth was the message, the child contestants obliged
To exercise the right energy and enterprise
To run themselves briskly through the board's intricate arrangement
Of pleasure, danger, and delight without risk,
Their assignment to luck into opportunities
That would set off crescendos of bells ringing,
Video *paradisos* of lights flashing through the transparent Lucite
         under their feet.

Yet it was splendor and the minute articulations of a fantasy village's architecture
That mesmerized me, that a child could skip along in a moment's time
Without having to be put in a car or be handled by adults,

To a candy store, movie house, or shop full of cream puffs.
Glee and surprise were everywhere just on the next luminous square
Around the looping turn on the glittering game board.

When the power went out one day, or perhaps when the show was canceled,
I got out scissors, paper, and pens, Crayolas arranged in stick puddles
On the dingy, carpeted floor of the apartment's living room,
Mapping out a village of my own on wax paper from a kitchen drawer.
I found empty green stationery boxes my mother brought home from work,
Tore the labels off, drew on them, marked rectangles for doors;
I cut windows, made folding blinds, used the leftover cutouts
To make counters and tables, a long, folded cardboard flume
For water to run in a sluice . . . the *tōfu*-maker, the rows of shacks,
A union hall where my uncles would gather, my aunt's gas station
On the highway, clear glass medicine bottles for pumps,
The peaked roof of Kahuku Betsu-In, the barber's, the butcher's,
The Chinese Association . . .

      This was the village we left behind—
And our apartment, the scatter of debris on its floor, my child's ark
         of the lost world.

II

THE WARTIME LETTERS OF HIDEO KUBOTA

Kubota to Miguel Hernández in Heaven, Leupp, Arizona, 1942

The sun travels slowly from over the top of this adobe stockade

And, when I finally wake and pull my face to the bars

At my window, I see a gray light filling in the shadows

Between the mess and guard quarters

And among river stones on the sides of the central well.

Horses snort and whinny far off from the corral I cannot see,

And a line of burros shuffles by, led by a single Navajo

Dressed in khaki-colored clothes from the trading post.

I've been here two months now, can name the hills

Surrounding this plateau of piñon pines—words I learned

From the guards and other prisoners, Japanese like me

Swept up in the days after the attack on Pearl Harbor.

The guards won't say what our crime is, rarely address us,

But I overhear them sometimes, saying the names of mountains,

Nearby towns, complaining about food and us "Japs."

They won't say if we'll be let go. The interrogators come

Every few days and ask about our hobbies back home—

Studying poetry, working the shortwave radio at night,

And me, how I go night fishing for *kumu* on Kahuku Point.

What landed me here was I used to go torching,

Wrapping the kerosene-soaked rags on bamboo poles,

Sticking them into the sand inside the lagoon,

And then go light them with a flick from my Zippo.

The fish come in from outside the reef,

Schooling to the light, and me I catch enough

To feed my neighbors—Portagee, Hawaiian, Chinee, and all—

Eating good for days after, like New Year's in early December.

For this they say I'm signaling submarines offshore,

Telling the Japanese navy the northernmost landfall on the island.

That's a lie. They ask when—I tell them. They ask where—I tell them.

How many fish?—I tell them same every time. No change my answer.

But how can you transform your sorrow into poems, Miguel?

To think of your wife and infant son with only onions to eat,

While you sing your lullabies from your cell in Alicante?

Is it cold for you, Miguel? With only the dark to wrap yourself in?

It is warm, even hot here on Navajo land in northern Arizona,

Where your poems descend to me in the moon's sweet, silver light

As it rises over the Mogollon Plateau these summer evenings.

They say that your sentence was death for writing poetry,

That you celebrated the Republic and the commoners.

I celebrated only my family and the richness of the sea.

My sentence, therefore, is only eternity to wait, not knowing,

Imagining *everything,* imagining nothing—

My wife taking in boarders, doing their laundry and sewing,

My children growing more trivial by the day

Without word where I have been taken,

Whether I will be returned or simply have vanished

Into the unwritten history of our country.

Your suffering tells me to be patient, Miguel,

To think of your song of sweet onions lulling your baby,

Even in his hunger, to a peaceful sleep,

While the wars of our time, and their ignorant ministrations,

Go on shedding their black, tyrannical light into the future.

Kubota to Nâzim Hikmet in
Peredelkino, Moscow, from Leupp, Arizona

I learned a sheepherder's stew last week, Nâzim.

Navajos taught me to make it from scraps

Of lamb from the mess, onions from the army's bags,

And pine nuts I picked from the piñon trees on the walks

They allow me from time to time.

                        Hawks circling above,

A stray's carcass on the ground crawling with maggots,

A patch of mesquite, and blue clouds like Portuguese men-of-war

Stringing tentacles of rain across the far distance of the red-rock

                                  plateau around me.

I think of home too much, allow sorrow to swell in my throat

Whenever I hear the chatter of finches or the whirr of chukar flushed from the sages.

I recall my days hiding in stands of strawberry guava,

Hunting for plover in the grassy patches along the low ridges of the Ko`olaus

                              above the cane fields.

My 12-gauge made me feel I owned property like I was *haole,*

My shots with it brought down dinners of wild game for Sunday table.

Walking back home, down through the grass fields for cattle,

Jumping the irrigation ditches and sluices like a *luna wai,*

I felt like I was boss of things, a manager, and could dream any future,

Quiet cane fires in my heart, fresh mountain rains washing clean

    all the confusions of the day.

But when they slop me like I was pig and shove me

Into this dusty cell with no floor but the desert,

I can think of nothing but the pain of this dull light

Leaking in through the bars of my cell window,

And I hear the grind of a Jeep stalled in mud,
Or the shallow peeps of beggar birds asking for crumbs
From the guards and the innocent, passing Navajos
Going in and out of the post with their daily ease,
Murmuring their soft language of chuffs and whispers.

How can a man move from splendor to prison so swiftly
And learn to nurse his own soul in this abandonment?
You chronicle by the day, Nâzim, all the things you have loved—
The lacing touch of your wife's fingertips across your lips,
The fall of her veil across her face, your blue Polish eyes,
The tea you drink in little cups with her in the afternoons,
The quiet bells and padding of footsteps on a merchant street.

You sweeten the tenderness of your own soul in isolation, Nâzim,
In the face of accusations, in answer to questions from the unforgiving.
To a slap, you return a smile; to a fist, you give a kiss; to torturers,
You write poems planning the planting of an olive tree when you are seventy!

My way adds a little pain each day, though my captors are not rough.
They give me potatoes, toss me their leftover fruits, light my cigarette.
But I quail like a bird when I think too much, fluttering in my soul
The escaping wings that are the withering of hope and who I used to be—
Proud father and storekeeper, husband to Tsuruko,
And grand keeper of loans and accounts for Lā`ie village.

*

I can give no tenderness to myself within these walls,
Only scratch my name and quote a saying from a poem
On the day the DOJ first brought me here to Leupp.

When you saw the blue sky that one day in Istanbul, Nâzim,
How could you lie down on the ground and look up to it
In respectful devotion to its full immensity?

                                        Teach me this—
To think only of the white wall I lean on next to me,
As you did, to forget Anatolia, your home, and Hawai`i, mine,
To grieve only for an instant for the waves of the seas we have lost,
For the freedom and the preciousness of our lonely wives.
Teach me the soil, Nâzim, the sun and the time, as babies,
Born in strife, that they first took us into it.

Kubota Writes to José Arcadio Buendía

There was no history in your village, as there wasn't in mine,
Until the day a B-17 circled over us, turning at Lā`ie Point,
And forgoing the water landing in the lagoon by the Beauty Hole,
Clipping the Cook pines by hole no. 9 and the Filipino graves,
To land, big as a green-brown whale, on Kahuku Golf Course.
It was a miracle like ice for you, a hole in reality a Gypsy brought
So that you could stick your finger into it, rip it large, and see
What might be the future that had only you and your forgetfulness
As the past from which to derive its phantasms of pain and glory.
We, on the other hand, though mesmerized as you, wanted for nothing
Except story—a window like a pathway to the world beyond us—
For we could already see we were surrounded by the aquamarine of seas,
Our world a deathlessness between the splashes of wave and wind.
And so we ran down our dirt Jeep roads, across dunes piled by the shore,
Betweens stones marking the collected dead of our *kumpadres* in the cane fields,
And onto the stubbly greens of what we'd made for our leisure joy—
A nine-hole set of golf links set beside the sea on sandy ground.

I saw it was a plane, lowest in the sky and with American markings,
A bomber with its frame speckled with bullet holes and rudder shot ragged,
Smoke from its hydraulics trailing like a kite's blue-gray tail, a long smudge
over the choppy sea.
It was the first any of us had seen up close, though, and we wanted
To touch it as if it were a newborn thing we had to wash and wonder over.

When it landed, I was on the batcher just above the ditch from the piggery,
And I could see it heave like a frigate bird as it touched down,
Making a sound, not like a creature of air, but like a bucket
Full of nails and screws being set down on a scrabbly beach of stones—
Metallic, heavy, and with a weight out of scale with our knowing.

*

People ran towards it, streaming through the cane fields like mice
Fleeing a burning, but they stopped and made a hushed circle around it,
Maybe thirty feet away, children kneeling down and crawling forward
For closer looks, women straightening their muslin dresses, men
In khakis and straw hats, boots caked with mud and bagasse,
Glancing towards each other as if to ask, *Who will possess this dream?*

I saw my wife among them, down by the narrow neck of a green fairway.
I recognized her from the neat swirl of her black hair against her head,
The cotton *muumuu* she'd sewn from Botan rice sacks, peonies
At her shoulders like epaulets, yellow butterflies across her bodice.
She held her hands clasped, as if in sleep or prayer, against the side of her face,
And the wind furled around her like current flowing through fingers of coral.

I felt tied to a tree, as you were, José, and wanted to reach my arms out towards her,
But nothing but horror moved within me as the hatch door was flung open
And the young airman hurled himself through, tumbling to the sandpatchy grass,
Hitting his shoulder, then lying like a green and brown octopus tangled in its own limbs,
Not moving but heaving, all of us forestalling our futures in this brief immobility.

What came next was nothing magical—from this miracle no astrolabe was gifted to me
To present further mysteries and delights. No lifelong friend with alchemy in his soul,
Magnets in his kit, or tales of esoteric cabals that knew secrets of the afterlife.
It was a captain who came, filling the opened hatchway with his large shadow.
He was holding something, and, from the flap of leather attached to his leg,
I knew it would be a pistol, which he pointed towards my gathered neighbors,
Who flinched and took steps backward, then stopped as soon as he spoke.

The engines had ceased their coughing by then and nothing but the soughing of wind
Through ironwood trees came through to me, though I could see he'd ordered them.

*

No one moved after that, and the captain swung himself from the plane to earth

Like a sloth swings from a tree limb to the leaf-littered floor of a forest.

It was gymnastic and nonchalant, something I might've admired, had the bile of fear

Retching up in me not been there, as the man staggered towards his comrade

Lying on the green, jittering the pistol in his shaking hand like a landing strut.

What he shouted then I could hear clearly. It was the name we'd all be called

From that day on, an epithet made ready in the Mainland papers I'd read as wrappings

On farm tools and aluminum cookware that I stocked in the plantation store.

Japs! he'd said, and it would be the word that brought us, the ignored and isolate,

Into the history of the world to number among its wretches, ripped from our villages,

No longer who we were to each other, but who these others needed us to be for their rage.

Kubota to the Chinese Poets Detained on Angel Island

In memory of Him Mark Lai

My geography does not match yours, surrounded by the bay
And the city so close by you can see it from the hill of Island.
I am at the middle of an ancient sea, raised up out of water
To make a dusty land of red and pink rock, yellow cliffs,

                        and snow peaks

Far from the Great Ocean you crossed from your home villages.

But we spend our days alike—gazing at bare walls,
Composing poems to carve on them, bedding down at night
To the whistling of wind through bars and barracks.
When the moon shines and insects chirp under our bunks,
Grief and bitterness wrap around us like cold, winding sheets,
And we rage against the whites and the promises
This land made to us it would be a heaven of gold mountains.

Hard living through confinement—our families not near,
Interrogators trying to catch us in stories
That do not match what your immigration papers say,
That do match lies informants have said about me.

Can you remember how many steps to the duck pond?
How many houses were south of the village well?
Which order brother died in the Year of the Ox?

They ask me about the ink stone and the radios in my house
The FBI took on December 8, about the military school
I attended in Hiroshima, though I was born in U.S. like them.

We try to act bravely, as we were taught, chests full of blood.
But we are not heroes. The wild geese of the bay echo your cries,
The coyotes mimic mine, and only ghosts escape these places,

Rising from the cold bodies of men who hang like butchered meat
In the lavatories, pale lights shining through the thin gauze
                                        of their clothes.
They will see their families, but only from the clouds.
I pity them, but share my dreams with you, poets of Island,
Trapped beneath the guard towers of history.

When they ask you your brother's name, say *It is Kubota.*
When they ask me what light attracts the fish at night,
I will answer *The light of angels from Island.*
When they ask what fish come to the light,
I will say *A fish that swims the River of Heaven.*

Kubota Returns to the Middle of Life

Coming back, I've been helped by the lessons you have taught, Tadeusz,
That a man's task is not only to rebuild a country,
But his own household, and even more the *spirit* of home,
Of wife, of meat and rice, of lights on at night
And no one slamming shut the door that locks you in.

This is bread, you told me as I smoked in my cell, *this is life.*
And I said, *Yes, this is Kubota's life*—to live near the sea,
To harvest from its garden, to sharpen a knife
In the back room of my store and walk out of my door
And hold the blade up to the sun so I could see it shine.

This is a man, you said. *A man's life is important—*
It is of the highest importance. And it was my mantra
Every moment I felt my heart shrink back small as a walnut,
Black and withered with the fear of a man who was a number.

I created myself after my death, Tadeusz,
I constructed life with desert and memories of home.
This is a window, you told me, and I gazed beyond it
To the future where a garden awaited me with my wife in it
Holding in her arms the pink and yellow blossoms from plumeria trees.

The blossoms fell, Tadeusz, fell from her arms heavy with scent
As she swayed in the music of all the objects of life.
It was my welcome home—my sons shy and awkward, not yet men;
My grown daughters laughing and weeping; one of the old villagers
Pulling a goat by a rope and giving me its life as tribute
To my silence, years long, and refusal to betray them.

*

This is a man this is a tree this is bread,
You have taught me. *People nourish themselves in order to live.*
And I ate what was given for the sake of returning to the midst of life,
So I could talk to the water, so I could stroke the waves in the lagoon with my hand,
So I could converse with the river running through our village
Past cane fields down to the fishponds and out over the reef.

Our lives are of great importance! I shouted to my wife
When I returned to her arms of plumeria blossoms;
Human life is important, as I talked to the water
And the moon and the flowers.

This is Kubota, I said to the earth, to the rain.
And if I heard a voice flowing from the sky, the earth, or the sea,
Tadeusz, it was a stubborn one from the threshold of your house.

Kubota Meets Pablo Neruda on the Street

Under the separated leaves of shade of the yellow *hau* tree,
The old one that has existed unchanged longer than any other
Tree in our village, I walk behind a huge *haole* man
In a white linen suit, his head balding and close-cut on the sides.
He pulls from his pants pocket a gaudy handkerchief,
Its persimmon-orange silk billowing like a schooner's sail
In the momentary wind, then mops his glistening brow with it.
He sways slightly, gazing up the dirt street to the taro fields
Blazing in sunlight, green elephant ears of leaves
Trembling in neat rows nearly all the way to the Ko`olau.

He walks through air the rain has washed, a boat of a man
Moving easily on the bright foam of white leather shoes,
Seeming to me miraculous, the gigantic swan from a child's tale
Shaking off the remnants of its adult birth,
Slicking his wet hair, combing it back, winding and rolling
The iridescent scarf around the great dampness of his neck.

I have seen the egglike face in photographs before,
Heard of his exiles to an island in Italy and to Mexico,
Read of his own brief imprisonments and escape on mule back
Once across the Andes, only to suffer arrest again,
His guard gifting him, though, with his own poem in tribute.
I too have read Neruda's poems, heard them recited in my own jails
By the janitors in Santa Fe, by the soldiers in Albuquerque.
Salt of the roads and *oceanic eyes* Neruda sings,
A beach of *disseminated sorrows, of nocturnal sugars*
                              ransomed with blood.
I wanted to say to him *My cemeteries are not lonely!*
My graves are full of bones sighing with the waves from the sea!
But, with a wave of his immense hand, sulfur-colored birds,

39

His feet and his nails, his shirts from which slow, dirty tears
Are falling, choke off my words, and they settle like dust
Among the market greens and marine shadows of this street.

As I walk behind this man I remember that before I returned,
I walked the open desert at dawn outside my prison cell,
Following the whispers I heard come from birds in the sky,
From the slithering lizards on the loose sands of the earth,
And wished, only as desperate men wish, "May this day
Be different from the last!" Even as the birds mocked me,
Wishing as birds wish, with all the immensity of sky they inhabit,
"May this day be the same as your last, Kubota!"

But, when I see this great bird of a man, when his eyes
Meet my eyes, they bring a flower's shade from the *hau* tree,
The shade of a swan's wing, the coolness of early evening
                              in the middle of the day.

Speak to me, Pablo, arrive in my life like an admiral
Dressed for dinner, place on my face the fiery kiss
Of a brother liberated from oceanic pain, flying above
The sea as clouds do, cathedral-like, trailing translucent rains.

I walk faster, Pablo, catching up with you, beseeching you to turn.
I touch your great shoulder with the curl of my palm
Just as you glance back at me, and the gold of your brilliant teeth
Catches in the highest light of day.

                              You call out my name—
Camerado! And lift me off my feet in transcendent recognition,
Pure acceptance. And I cannot tell my life from yours, Pablo,
My suffering from your subterranean joy up from volcanic depths
Of molten rock and the sheer, underwater cliffs of the sea.

I rise up with you, American brother, from the deepest
Reaches of my crushed hope, I take up your feathered hands
Which lift me, like a great bird skimming lucent jewels
From the sea, into these new, fresh days of my vernal life.

Kubota on Kahuku Point to Maximus in Gloucester

Wind ruffling my shirt and pants, a gleam across the water,
Surf sounds in my ears, I roll the cuffs up my trousers,
Wade out in rubber-stockinged feet over the crags of black rock,
Sea-slick with foam and garlands of kelp, and pick my way across
Pockets of coarse sand, the crushed white corals in bits of brilliant grit
Beneath my steps, and realize I have had to learn the simplest things last:
Never to get angry, content each day with four bowls of rice,
Some vegetables, and my house and store under the shade of pines.

Ten years since the war's end and they sent me back.
Ten years of counting myself last in everything.
I was slow at first to put my hand out, to try and do the world's business.
I stood aloof from that which was most familiar,
Hurt by the drought of sympathy, cold in summer,
Defeated by rains in winter, the wind ever my better.

But I turned tack and ran with the shifting breezes one day,
No longer estranged, embraced by the lapping waves of the sea,
Content not that the land was behind me only,
But that I gave no longer my first thoughts to myself,
But to my village, to the mother who was weary
To whom I must carry a sack of rice, to nature's dialogues
With heaven, and to the lush fall of rains that darken,
Like blush on a woman's face, the waiting surface of the sea.

My trade, finally, was not in commerce with goods,
But an exchange with fear and burden—
My job to relieve them, going forth through sickness and argument,
Bringing a pear to one who is thirsty, a joke and the trick of silence
To the angriest man on the most sunless street in town.

*

But in no way am I wise. I have squandered my care
On useless things: the spoon I craved to sharpen to a chisel,
The lamp I prayed for to reach through the black milk of night,
The repair I sought for the worn tatter of my soul.

All these came with time and a change of wind—
War's end, my innocence again my own first possession.

So, today I look out as a wind and water man,
Unfurling the loose folds of my black net from its perfect geometry of stones
So it spreads like the shade from a monkeypod tree
Over the furtive edges of the lagoon, dropping down
On the green darts of fish and grasping them up in a ball
When I cinch from my wrist the tether and pull the whole, writhing thing up.

I know now the quarters of weather, when it comes,
Where I must go with it. Innocence is as ephemeral as that—
A cloud massing, unforeseeable, around the blade-edge of Ka`ena Point
One winter's night, a swarm of misfortune, then the slow peace again,
Fish running with the tide, a soft wind in your shirt pocket.

It is undone business that makes us most calm—
A pine grove's shade on a dune by the edge of the sea,
Coconuts and glass floats to gather bobbing from the surf.

It is to you, Maximus, I address myself this morning, across oceans
And the continent, with the sea stretching out from my feet.

III

THE ART OF FRESCO

PROLOGUE

As a boy growing up in Hawai`i, I felt among the most mysterious of relatives were the single men, many of whom were war veterans. They seemed to picture the world differently from the rest of us—we who laughed when we gathered, who came when called, who ate when served. They did not, but instead sat stolidly in bamboo easy chairs or perched on diner stools apart from us, sipping whiskey and beer, while the world of our frivolity spun around them. When they spoke, it was infrequently and usually only to each other as they sat in rough circles around coffee and card tables. And I remember a war buddy of theirs they called Fresco—a man so deeply tanned he was red as the dirt, who wore gold-rimmed spectacles and slept out under the hau trees at the beach park. He'd be there most days, sitting with his haunches and feet balanced on the calcareous cage of roots under a screwpine by the sea, sketching in a schoolboy's small tablet, the edge of its pages flapping in the winds. If I tried to interrupt him with pestering or by stealing a close-up glance over his shoulder at the scroll of waves he might be drawing, I'd be hushed and shooed away by an aunt, who would not explain.

Years later, in the fall of 1987, at an event at Arlington, Virginia, I was among men like these once again. It was a reunion at the National Cemetery of the 442nd Combat Team—the battalion of Japanese Americans who fought in Europe during World War II. Mostly in their late sixties and early seventies by then, they were gathered for a ceremony at the Tomb of the Unknown Soldier, then for speeches and a picnic in the Memorial Amphitheater. I was there to include them and their event in a magazine feature I was trying to write.

But so much of what they said could not be told in the language of reportage. And so much of what I felt could not either. All that silence and mystery about them I had carried in memory since I was a child would not dissipate. And there were some curious new facts they told me.

For one thing, many of the younger vets, who'd enlisted late during the war and who'd served as replacements for the first battle casualties at Salerno, Monte Cassino, and Anzio, were also late in mustering out and stayed on even after the war was over. They told me of their swift campaign soldiering along the Arno from Livorno to Scandicci, passing though Pisa and under its Leaning Tower. Of broken marble from statues littering the streets. They told stories of bivouacs up in the mountains above Florence the summer after the Italian surrender and days the army sent them down into the city for cooking school, art classes, and language lessons. "I saw Michelangelo's David because of World War II," one of them declared. "And I learn those days how for draw one pick-cha of nekkid gyirl!"

Their conversations swung easily from remembrance to jocularity in this way, steeped in the odd, alternately rueful and happy ironies of their lives during the war and shortly after it. In a moment they could move from laughter to tears and then beg my pardon when they wept, ever conscious of dignity. The fall sun shone brightly on both marble and flesh that day.

"The Art of Fresco" is a story of theirs.

1. THE EXPULSION

I was seventeen and fresh out of "Tokio High" in Honolulu.
It was 1943 and headlines of war had given us an adolescent ache for valor.
By '44, there were screams, explosions, and cries from men like frail geese,
A corporal blown to dirt and a dithering chaff of flesh,
Artillery's ghastly flowers blossoming up the hill we humped.
Later, silence and the dark, the stench of battle smoke and grief
Like whispers creeping over the hot, loosened ground.

I wanted the sea then, scalloped azure and aquamarine off Kahuku Point,
Wind's kind caress up my sleeves, the sun's fingers in my hair.
I thought memory would damn me, but it didn't,
Life again in a weekend pass to Florence and Michelangelo's *David*—
Naked, white, untouched by terror—magisterial above me, a lesson in mute stone.

Lost across the river one day,
The Arno we had trucked along from Pisa to Scandicci,
I entered a chapel's opened door and saw a garden without sin,
Then the apple and Eve's voluptuous snake of her own face,
Her love of Self displacing God's,
And then the aggrieved flight from earthly innocence.

I felt my own shame then, Masaccio,
Faithless and without gardens of my own,
No history and a people who had worked only the cane,
Salvation in the sweet arc of a cutter's blade.

If I pick one up now, *maestro,*
Let it swing like a big brush over layers of gigantic grasses,
Arriccio and *intonaco,* float and gloss coats,
And let the crop speak of their souls,
Sugared paints of this undulant, green sea.

Tiepolo's vault of sky, clouds like spun satin over the blue-gray

　　　　　　　　　　　　　　　　　　　　shimmer of sea,

I walked out day after day to this rotted bathhouse, a leftover

　　　　　　　　　　　　　　　　　　　　from the WPA—

Seven pillars, a central arch and hutch for concession sales and condiments,

Broken-down trellis and decrepit canopy over what was once an area

　　　　　　　　　　　　　　　　　　　　for picnics—

And I imagined a beachside *cappella,* showers for ablution, fountains for

　　　　　　　　　　　　　　　　　　　　the penitent.

It had been months since mustering out, barrages had blanked my memory,

And what I liked was the sighing wash of the sea dragging its grassy hair,

Its skeletal corals like finger bones across the chattering rocks of the shore.

I came at dawn and stayed till dark. I came at midnight and slept till light.

I brought charcoal and a sketch pad. I left it blank.

I wrapped myself in fronds I gathered from under the leaning funicular

Of a coconut tree, and sat one day staring at the sea.

Guns from Monte Cassino had flung a heavy fear our way.

Dug in for months before the assault by Company A,

Our orders to pull out came only after half our guys were gone.

I wanted something like seraphim,

Angels articulated in a banner of clouds scudding across the far horizon,

To come for me sailing from lavish sight to an inner blue,

Like warm, home waters bathing me inside out.

What *figurae* did I have? What iconography?

A bearded saint and his stippled aurora meant nothing,

Even in gold and lapis lazuli.

A body bulleted into bits was remembrance.

*

I wanted vision like an altarpiece I saw,
Saints in conversation around Madonna and Child,
These poor fishermen wading in the surf become my Magi,
Green mountains robed in rain my sacred conversation,
Annunciation in the pure rising of the sun.

When shadows blanched and an aubade of lights showered across my face,
I'll paint the walls, I thought. I'd trowel the cracks and lavish plasters.
I'd invite the sea, umbers of the earth, the limed pigments I'd brush
Would be coral roads through a frightful dark,
Dawn breaking on my own island at last, my symbols spare and cerulean.

Earth faces, umber and burnt sienna, halos of canvas and khaki
Swaddling their heads, peasant not priestly hands
Gloved against the slash of cane fibers,
The sugary brew of soil, crystals, and juice . . .

These make my typology, humble and not holy,
A GI's scratch pad and not Giotto's flat stone of Vespignano my tablet.
I needed a vocabulary of images—workers in the fields,
The locomotive and its sulfurous plume,
Curtains of rain against the velvet-green cliffs of the Ko`olau,
Its folded screen of stone the constant backdrop to sculpted dunes
And the scalloped sea I drew, a screwpine and its anemone'd tentacles
Of green winding through a yellow *hau* tree, on their way
Through wet ruffles of wind and up the empurpled squid-ink of sky
To the rayed promises of Avalokiteśvara's Paradise.

Ea, the Hawaiians sing when there's too much for saying.
And I never felt that way until I saw the North Shore again,
Europe weeks in the past, the Gothic Line still tangling up my speech.
Ea, when the first bird's-wing brushed my sight,
When the ten thousand crosshatch strokes of light
Began a silver shimmer beyond the surf I waded in.

I'll take cane fields and rain, I said,
Churning my unshrouded body about,
The running tide scumbling its shallow chop
In green convulsions of symmetry and pain.

"Zigaretten," the Nazi prisoner begged, and I gave him a Camel already lit,
Both of us sitting cross-legged on the hill outside Fiesole.
Downslope, Centro Storico and its blown bridges,
The Ponte Vecchio alone left intact, a mauve line
Of linked villas and terra-cotta pontoons smoking with burning trash.

War's end and what I wanted was to step inside San Marco again,
Stroll through its slow chambers of instruction, *istoria* in shuttered rooms,
Meditations in soft earth tones, blue enigmas of robes and sky,
Pea-green fronds of palms and an ochre and white-lime sepulcher of rock.

"No touch me, eh?" Ichiro said, leg off-angle, blood wetting
The green khaki darker on his chest. On the beach at Anzio,
Not one of us stayed in the boat. We jumped into the sea,
Waded ashore in that green-yellow light of my first Italian dawn.
I wondered if he was dead the moment I said, "Go For Broke."

Onto drying plaster, with a dressmaker's wheel, I incise a cartoon drawing
Of scores of village dancers in summer *kimono* waving paper fans,
The *ondo*-maestro perched in his tower, singing *min'yō* through a megaphone
Balanced on a tripod stand, *hayashi* of flute and drums seated right of him,
The *ō-daiko* a tan circle like a leather moon rising above them all.

With a pounce of charcoal, I dust the outlines of the *yagura* tower
And its wooden struts and rope lashings, then I trace
The bulky Japanese knots and a bamboo ladder that goes up its side.

Next, once the whole design is transferred to the plaster,
I paint in the first layer of wet colors, pounding down
On each of the faces and figures like a drummer,
And what I hear is an old music, priestly and pentatonic,
Guiding my strokes as it instructs the dancers in their moves, step and pose,
A gesture of the extended hand held over my father's bandannaed head
As if a silver hemicircle of moon were rising
Behind an intricate calligraphy of tattered clouds,
Sora's *hokku* for the solstice written over a field of decorative stars
Thick as luminous milk from Aldebaran across the River of Heaven.

This is Bon Odori, the Festival of the Dead,
And it was my joy to catch the sway of rhythmic bodies
Wrapped under light cotton prints and sleeves like flags
They twirled and fluttered as they danced like yellow moths
In my paints, clothing simpler than bare flesh to render *a fresco.*

A soldier's face then, whitened in lime,
Hung like the torn paper of a lantern at the edge of things,
Figura to be, premonition and ghost ship of terror amidst flotillas of joy.
Save him, I say. Let his soul leap from its passion to the farther shore.
Bodhi . . . svāhā . . . His father will be there, showing him the way,
Stretching out his hand, the opposite one from which extends

an afterlife bloom of fan.

6. CANE FIRES

Lit torches in the fieldworker's hands,
A Scot *luna* to the side directing them,
Pointing with the butt end of a whip,
Set it here . . . Set it there . . .

Someone spotting oil along the rootstocks,
Small lanterns of orange licking up stalks
Still green, unflamed, short-swords of leaves
Chittering in the constancies of wind.

They've cleared a space, a small *piazza*
Amidst the cane, where a driver brings
His string of several mules, hides gleaming in the sun.
In the yellow foreground, a mother sits and opens up
The moiled blouse of her *kimono* so she can nurse a child.

I do them in browns, touches of black
With a fine brush, glosses of sienna,
A squiggle of red, acidic earth.
Smoke and ash I'll add later,
Gray-blues and umbers, benign infernos.

7. BAPTISM

Sada and I rode the half-track down the wooded hills,
Then the truck through the mountain road and village checkpoints
To Florence, where the army had us going to school.
Postwar, it was hot and dry that summer and the Jerries we guarded
Were all getting shipped out. I didn't want to go home myself,
But to fill in the blank thoughts that had suddenly bloomed in my mind
After I saw San Marco and all the monks' chambers there,
Each wall given its own scene—soft robes and colors like powder
Inlaid on a hard plaster, cool even in the mid-August heat.

My breath went still and still again as I passed from cell to cell,
Telling myself the story not of Christ, his miracles, and final travail,
Nor of the loyal retinue of disciples, each face its own beatitude,
But of the friars who painted them, devoted, swimming wet brushes
From bare flesh to holy road, carving Angelico's designs on wet plaster,
Blackening a sketch with powders of a charcoal made from a willow tree.
For it was no spirit or story that grabbed me first, but the form
Of the art itself and the pure devotion of the patient man who made it,
Shapes and colors of sanctity like flowers from an untorn ground.

After war, it was what I sought myself—a coolness of mind
And a notion large enough to fill the future and all its rooms.
I spent each leave sketching in the chapels—Santa Maria Novella,
Santa Croce, and the Cappella Brancacci across the Arno—
And I tried to train myself in the language of light and shadow,
The geometries of form and composition, the torso's inverted pyramid,
Globes and architectural lines of perspective, background landscapes.

It was my own great unknowing I wanted to fill, the vapor of a cloud
Across the silver visage of the full moon, tangible and evanescent at once.
I knew and I did not know and the undecidable difference was inspiration

That kept me dressed in khakis past the war's end, hands smudged
With Florentine *verdiccio,* head bowed over the sketch pad
Like the penitent being baptized, kneeling in a transparent stream,
St. Peter bathing his stringy hair with water from a plain, wooden bowl.

8. THE APSE OF APPRENTICESHIP

A gruff Florentine was my teacher, who caught me gazing over his shoulder,
Not so much at his images nor even the loveliness of his patterns and designs
On the sketch pad he was working that morning in San Marco,
But at the speed, deftness, and exhilaration of his strokes,
The limber wrist calibrated for the gentle, flowing calligraphy
Of the knife-cut pencil's swift travel across the rough surface of the paper.

There to add his paints to that of Ghirlandaio and Beato Angelico,
He gave me an address in the neighborhood north of Santa Croce—
Via Fiesolana, 34—and invited me by to observe him teach.
I went the next morning and saw six starving adolescent boys,
Most dressed in scavenged clothes and still stinking from foraging garbage,
A single beatific glance rolling like a wave across each of their faces
As I passed among them, going easel to easel, until I found
My own place, an empty slot on the semicircle they made,
Arranged around the live, sitting model, the ribs along her back
As exposed as the slats of charred wood on the wall she leaned against.
At the break, in front of us all, she sipped from a holstered GI canteen,
And, in my breath, I could feel the pebble grains of its green denim cloth.

Like Sada, I was supposed to be in cooking school near San Lorenzo,
Learning broths and reductions, how to make a proper charcoal
And lay the brick in convection patterns for a wood-fired stove.
But it was pencil drawings and plaster casts the Florentine had me study,
Values of light and shade, halftone scales, volumes of spheres and cylinders
That comprised the human body, its fundamental vocabularies of form.
I grew to love that an unsharpened strut of charcoal could whisper
As it skimmed across the rough paper I tacked to a plywood easel
And capture both the white glaze of ceramic and the soft murk
Of shadows pooled beneath the eyes of a chivalric bust.

*

I learned I was not to draw but to conjure highlights and subtle fluctuations
Where my hand lifted away from the gessoed and gouached papers
Rather than striking them, and it was as though, throughout all my soldiering,
I'd been caught downlooking, deep in the olive darks of a sea-cliff cove
And it was just now that I slowly revolved my face and torso upwards
Toward the golden streaks of light striking the surface of the waters
That pulsed in arabesques and made a luminous apse above me.

9.   ROOFSCAPE

Bicycles and Moto Guzzis filled the cobblestone streets through the city
But there was barely any rubble, each wall intact, statues still standing.
I took cigarettes, a sketch pad, and went up on a rooftop on Via San Gallo
So I could strip to my undershirt and skivvies in the August heat,
Look out across the roofscape to the Duomo and Giotto's Campanile,
Then north to the forested hillsides of Fiesole where we'd once camped.

If I could see the Arno, it might be a shard of silvered aquamarine
                                                    in the summery light.
If I could see westward to where we'd trucked three nights from Pisa,
I'd look away, back to Brunelleschi's egg-shaped, terra-cotta dome,
And imagine the artist struggling with flying arcs and intricate designs
Until everything flowed from a single idea, a shape that shimmered
On the edge of thought like light reflecting off the back of a fish
Finning quietly in the river's current, dodging flotsam and debris,
While children lobbed stones from the bank and the fouled waters
Rushed silently by, never touching the bronze, herringbone pattern of skin.

I made a sketchbook of studies as soon as I was home:
Jiichan driving his mule across the village garden patch,
Ploughing up the earth, rows of shacks visible in the background,
A *poi* dog scratching itself in the dirt street, while a flock of kids
Chased after a cane truck, one stooping to pick up a dropped stalk,
And, over them all, a waft of soot from the mill stack
Spreading like a long, slim banner of black gauze across the page.

It was a form of penance that I practiced, earning up the patience,
Like Angelico's, I told myself, for what I envisioned was ahead,
Storing up the small piles of alms I knew I must have
To make within myself, and out of yearning, these raw images
And a steadiness of practice borrowed from common life—
A bust of Babasan in a shaft of yellow window-light in the kitchen,
Sewing at the table, stitching together a muslin apron of old rice sacks;
A way with paints, whether oils or temperas, that had the turning
Of a wooden wheel in it, the stoop-and-stand rhythms of hoe-*hana* laborers
Chopping dirt in the dry fields before the seed-cane was planted;
That, if my brush were to drink in a pure red from the palette I'd prepared,
It would not lay itself down as an ocher or terra rosa,
But as the burnt skin on a stalk of cane or the scowling face of a waterman
Crouching over the jammed gate of his muddy, grass-fouled sluice.

I tramped out over the irrigation ditches and old mule-tracks
To Gang no. 7 and watched them as they found shade
Against a stand of cane, broke for lunch, and crouched over
Their aluminum meal pails, slurping cold rice as if it were soup,
Sucking from their chopsticks the greasy juices left there
From their brown-sauced meats and yellow pickles.
A round-faced one, with his mouth opened in a howl

Like one of Goya's tortured peasants, shoveled in the sugared beef.
A narrow-faced and bearded one held up and shared
The string of paper dolls his daughter had crafted the day before in school.
Four others, more shapes than faces, crouched around them,
One glancing back over his shoulder as if hearing a work whistle.

Raw umber was the color of the tilled earth that surrounded them,
Viridian the cliffsides of the Ko`olau that rose above their pause from labor,
And cadmium blue the undisturbed, quiescent bowl of the sea.
Paint was the past and all our comings—the long gaze of an immigrant
Debarking the first steamship and stepping onto shore.
Over his shoulder, slung across his back, the burden
Of a bronze silken bundle not yet marked with regret,
And the misting wash I sprayed over it, a faint *imago* of the future.

11. *IN MEMORIAM*

From Hau`ula I took the bus,
Kam Highway past La`ie to Kahuku,
And got off by the Castle & Cooke sugar mill,
Cane trucks grinding their gears,
Loads of cane piled in brown dunes by the dirt and gravel road
Oiled down against the devils and streams of wind.

It's been weeks since I knew I had to make this trip,
Take the sandy trail past the plantation store and vegetable stand,
Wind behind the ramshackle union hall,
Step out to the open dust of the square by the gray Hongwanji
And along the narrow pig-streets
To the shacks and papaya patches of the village.

I stop outside the wooden gate worn smooth and silvered by the rains,
Take a breath, and walk in the mossy yard abloom with bougainvillea,
Its scarlet hearts trellised up the sides of the shotgun shack.

Off to the side, little hillocks of manure;
Garden rows of cucumber, lettuce, and squash;
A scarecrow of sun-bleached rice bags
Crucified on a bamboo cross.

When I announce my name, calling at the door,
Two worn faces come into its long rectangle of sun,
Glance in recognition, and then their bodies begin to bow.
And I to them, handing across the thin threshold
A *lei* of dogtags and plumeria flowers.

A backdoor bangs from a neighbor's yard,
A small gong goes off in my head,
And my heart begins its sutra chant,
Ashes and cane dust and a slant of sun
Falling down on my suit and on my shoes.

12. *GIORNATA*

I saw her gathering *limu,* purple weeds from the sea,

Wading out in the shallows, hiking up her wrap

So it hugged her knees. But, when she bent,

Dipping down as if to smooth the undulant clear waters

With the soft spade of her hand, a banner of yellow and black silk

Spun like the furl of a trailing fin from a Moorish Idol

Making its slow parade among the broken corals

                                 and through the surf.

A net bag, dark green as the depths of the sea,

Was slung across her shoulder, made a transect

Across her chest so I could see the swells of her sensuousness

Pressed against the wet cloth of her simple blouse

When she turned to put her back against the breaking waves.

Though I watched her like this for minutes at a time

As she collected and cleaned bits of sand

From her fresh bunches of drenched salad from the sea,

Then stretching to the hour the plaster would no longer accept paint,

I never saw the briefest dance of a smile play across her face

Nor a glint of sun or spray from the topmost spinning curl of a wave

Make her expression turn from what seemed to me a gloom

That welled from a depth within, constant and unmoved

By sea and sky, the vault of clouds, the cry that began its ache

Within my own mute throat as I clenched the paints

From my brushes and readied myself for the long day's work.

13. MOANA

"Moana" means the sea and she knew its codices,

Manuscripts in every roll and shift of current,

The patterning of sand at the bottom of the lagoon

A folio page to read regarding weather and the coming tide.

She showed me a tiny cove, where she gathered shrimp

In small ponds she prepared with brine she dipped from the open sea,

Was once enclosed by a long jetty of river and mountain rock—

A farm for fish Hawaiians knew to raise, domesticated,

Tame as geese they could call for an evening's meal.

Their green and silver backs would glide through a raised weir

That opened a blue cut in the black-and-tan line of gigantic stones.

Fattened, called with a chant or whisper or a roil of food

Scattered like a beggar's loose change on the surface of the sea,

The fish would come, romanced by simple repetition

And the grand design of necessity and tropical cunning.

She showed me how a mullet swims from moving shadows,

How turtles bob at the reef's mouth until a rise of tide

Brings them streaming through a chute and tumbling into the bay.

We swam at sunset, following the long, green slope of a curl

When a school of darting fishes threaded through its face,

Silver needles and trails of stitchery embroidering

The comb and cuff of the wave. I felt love for her

When we reached dry land, Moana taking up her skirt

And folding it like a double screen around her hips,

Catching each wing of the red cloth with her elbows,

Its hemmed ends in each of her hands, closing first

The panel of the Pietà—two cranes sporting beyond

A jagged line of pine; then the Adoration—a trio

Of grottoed rocks on a shore of gold-painted ground.

The gift of a next-door neighbor from Japan, she said,

Innocent as dawn breaking the black of the night-cloaked sea.

The war was hard on those who waited too,
Moana said, untying the knotted *furoshiki,*
Revealing the lunch of cold, broiled fish
She had brought, passing me its pickles and *poi,*
The gray paste of it wrapped in a leaf of tī.
She did laundry and sewing for a *haole* boarder
Her family took in, a soldier from Schofield
Stationed at the airstrip near Tanaka Store.
From Philadelphia, an Italian named Digrasso,
"And he was nice," she said, bedding down with her
After a long walk through whispering canes
Where they told their secrets, the tender grasses
Speaking softly over their sighs. After a while,
He was sent away. She got a card posted onboard a troopship
Bound for Saipan. She never heard from him again,
Though the village knew she was great with a child
Due that spring. Her parents gave that girl away
To relatives on Moloka`i—an island Moana could never see
Even if she climbed up past where the trails end
On the barren mountain ridges to old *heiau*
And lookouts where Hawaiians once surveyed the sea.
"I hear she's pretty and *akamai,*" Moana said,
"Sharp as can be," and then glanced upwards
At my own paint-spattered face, a humble brim
Of tears barely trembling at the lips of her eyes,
Glaucous as she reached to clasp my hand,
Bringing it to her cheek, wet with its soft, warm rain.
"Today she would be three," she said, then shook away
My kiss, stood up, and refused to share more pain.

From the left edge, I painted first the high,
Cold wind gust that flattened the soft chop on the sea,
Then the flight of gulls and cormorants inland,
And sandpipers huddling under fallen trees.
There was no single, leading edge of cloud
Reddened and backlit by a sunset's light,
But a black, massing stack of them
Streaking wide across a far horizon.

In the middle of my panel,
I made the seas boil and pitch up
Scores of white tongues licking upwards
At the blank, cold currents of air,
And I painted not a storm but a hurricane.

Paniolo jumped from cattle boats and skiffs,
Heads bobbing like glass floats loose in the sea,
And steers swam like frightened, paddling dogs
Trying to make their way from deep water to shore
Like soldiers in the ocean off Anzio
Who made a slow, desperate crawl to the beach.

Most of the time, painting has worked,
Given me more than just what to do.
My eyes have risen back into my own face,
And I've given myself over to the tiny,
Significant tasks of each day. Once a week,
I hitch to Hale`iwa, then ride the pineapple truck
Up the Wahiawā plateau, choking on the red dust,
Eating diesel fumes and batting back pineapple bugs
Just to fetch fresh water for my paints.
I go above the agricultural spray zone
Where I know the fertilizer creeps into the reservoir,

And hike up past the town and hot fields

Down the gullies and groves of *haole koa*

To the foot of Mount Ka`ala where I begin my climb.

Up there is where the best water comes

In a rocky spring up from the ground

Covered with mosses and mists in the mornings

You'll see if you sleep there overnight.

I bring two big army canteens and fill them,

Putting their mouths to the boils and ripples in the stream;

But it's too hard to hear that much richness of silence for long,

And the clouds are so cool up there, you wonder

If you've joined the ghosts in Paradise.

It's a soul's leap they say, a platform

To make your jump to heaven—nothing there

Beyond the sloping ramp of the mountain's end—

No more island and nothing but sky.

Moana calls me back, though, and the paintings too,

My walls not yet finished but nearly so,

A sunburst to draw, cartoons of spinach and lychee

To transfer from perforated paper to plaster.

I slipped the silk from her shoulders one day,

Tasted the close, warm scents of her hair,

Her body like a taut, thick wing tucked against me,

And it was our vow to the salt winds of the sea,

To the blooming freshets of stream water

Flowing windward from land to the outer reef of the lagoon.

That crevice of life I'd been hiding within,

That wreckage of a bridge bombed by war's fires

That had been my constant home, I could walk away from now

In the daily crouching of my flesh towards hers,

In her feather's touch on my sun-warmed skin.

Whatever grief I have, there is a paint I can see

That burnishes it, brown to cinnabar in a stroke.

If I paint blue, I see the cadmium aura surrounding it.

I am a man. *How do I live? I live . . .*

With enough beach sand in my soul to fill a seacoast,

With an ocean of images to paint, roiling by the day,

In fresh hues brushed on a broken wall washed clean by time.

DEPARTMENT OF COMMERCE—BUREAU OF THE CENSUS

FOURTEENTH CENSUS OF THE UNITED STATES: 1920

POPULATION—HAWAII

County _Honolulu_
Island _Oahu_
District _Koolauloa_

NAME OF CITY, TOWN, OR VILLAGE _____

NAME OF INSTITUTION _Kahuku Plantation Co._

ENUMERATED BY ME ON THE _23_ DAY OF _January_ 1920 _Lloyd E. Young_ ENUMERATOR.

ENUMERATION DISTRICT No _70 A_
WARD OR DISTRICT OF CITY

PLACE OF ABODE	NAME	RELATION	TENURE	PERSONAL DESCRIPTION	CITIZENSHIP	EDUCATION	NATIVITY AND MOTHER TONGUE — PERSON / FATHER / MOTHER	OCCUPATION
203 384 341	Isano, Michai	Servant					Hawaii	
200 382 342	Sugimoto, Katsutaro	Head	R	M W 44 M			Japan — Japanese / Japan / Japan	Sugarmill
	, Tsuyoko	Wife		F W 44 M			Japan — Japanese / Japan / Japan	none
	, Jiro	Son		M W 14 S			Hawaii / Japan / Japan	none
	, Jumbo	daughter		F W 12 S			Hawaii / Japan / Japan	none
	, Iwaho	daughter		F W 10 S			Hawaii / Japan / Japan	none
	, Masamoto	Son		M W 3 S			Hawaii	none
	, Katsuko	daughter		F W 2 S			Hawaii	none
201 383 373	Rodriguez, Manuel	Head	R	M W 22 M			Hawaii / Japan / Japan	Sugar mill
205 384 344	Souto, Eliseo	Head		M W 37 M			Japan — Japanese / Japan / Japan	Plantation
	, Elza	Wife		F W 37 M			Japan — Japanese / Japan / Japan	none
	, Luih	daughter		F W 13 S			Hawaii / Japan / Japan	none
	, Miele	Son		M W 11 S			Hawaii / Japan / Japan	none
	, Elena	daughter		F W 8 S			Hawaii / Japan / Japan	none
	, Musako	daughter		F W 5 S			Hawaii	none
	, Masaichi	Son		M W 2 S			Hawaii	none
206 385 345	Masaoka, Saroku	Head	R	M W 36 M			Japan — Japanese / Japan / Japan	Laundry
	, Yuki	Wife		F W 34 M			Japan — Japanese / Japan / Japan	none
	, Suyano	daughter		F W 13 S			Hawaii / Japan / Japan	none
	, Shito	daughter		F W 5 S			Hawaii / Japan / Japan	none
	, Kitsue	Son		M W 4 S			Hawaii / Japan / Japan	none
	, Nobert	Son		M W 2 S			Hawaii / Japan / Japan	none
207 386 346	Rochin, Rikki	Head	R	M W 43 M			Japan — Japanese / Japan / Japan	Laborer Sugarmill
	, Shino	Wife		F W 43 M			Japan — Japanese / Japan / Japan	none

IV

A MAP OF KAHUKU
IN OREGON

Kawela Studies

Drizzle of rain pattering on the dwarf palms, dark towers and blue parapets of clouds
Over the ruffled blue gingham of the sea, sweet scent of seawrack and fresh life
borne on the wind
That ambles along the sands and sticks of drift like a nosing *poi* dog
Wigwagging from the lava rock point along this thin scythe of a beach . . .

I'm home again, curling waves tossing their soaked white tresses to the skies,
Dropping them tendrilously around my ankles in a dancer's expert tease,
Pipers scooting like feathered gray race-cars accelerating ahead,
The shark's fin-and-tail in the surf the first plainsong of the morning,
Gloria of the bobbing turtle just offshore the second.

I came here once when I was nineteen and near fully a Mainland kid by then,
Slept shrouded on the beach in a GI-surplus mosquito net,
> smoked Camels and Marlboros
Days playing cards with cousins—nickel bets, peanuts, and *pidgin* all in the mix—
Dripping bottles of Primo beer our cold drink, raw fish salad our chaser.

Winter vacation sophomore year, I'd brought a blue Sears suitcase
filled only with books—
Joyce, Beckett, Kawabata, Tillich, and Buber. Novels and baby theology.
I found something in them that drew an ache out of my heart,
Poultices of words, *pharmakoi* of pages flecked with angelic particles of sand,
As I read madly on the beach, dawn to dusk, frigate birds and gulls
Squawking overhead like schoolmates inviting me to leave studies behind
And sail with them in the gay, gusting winds, seek Amaryllis in the shaded seas.

But the most I would do was plunge in the surf when it got too hot,
Then stroke out past the shorebreak to the dark ribbon of reef
a hundred yards out.
Along the way, warm waters would be sieved with the cool

From freshwater springs coming through the lagoon's sandy bottom.
I'd catch gray glimpses of mullet schools, yellow tangs, and eel-like,

spotted hīnālea—

Wrasses furling amid green corals and tentacled blooms of white anemones.
And, if I flipped myself over like a contrarian seal, disporting on my back
And wanting to wail with the unsayable, I didn't know how to,
Except that aching had turned to resolve, the sun's scorn to imperative suggestion
As I floated along, catching my breath, feeling the wind's cool fingers
Tantalize along my trunks and wet skin of my arms and hairless chest.

Signature of all things I am here to read, thought Joyce's Daedalus,
Channeling Plato, himself derived from Heraclitean mystics
And yet their proud, sophistic apostate.

Unlike them, I had a place but no stories,

No tradition except utter silence like the deeps that fell away offshore,
Sixty feet to sixty fathoms in a breath. What was there was more than mystery,
The dropoff past unportrayed even in lore and without unisonance,
The luminous and anecdotal cloaked in inky shrouds, absent my own conjured romances.

And yet the ache stayed, as if all the slate sky was a stone's weight on my chest,
Pressing me down beneath the waves for truth and a confession,
Pressure of the unspoken shorting my breath until vision and the epiphanic
Might distinguish themselves from delirium, sunshowers over the opened seas
An amber dazzle to the left of my rolling shoulder as I shrugged quickly over
And began my measured strokes back to the daedal shore.

Bugle Boys

As I am Kubota's voice in this life,

                 chanting broken hymns to the sea,

So also am I my father's hearing,

                 fifty-five now and three years shy of his age when he died,

My ears open as the mouth shells of two conchs, drinking in a soft, onshore wind.

In the fall of '63, at the end of our first year in Gardena, south of L.A.,

                 electrician that he was, he built his own home hi-fi—

Speakers out of parts from Scandinavia, an amp kit ordered through the mails,

The glittering turntable, brushed aluminum painted gold, a belt drive, and an inboard motor—

Each component meticulously laid out on a bedsheet soon after it arrived,

Jigsawed cabinet boards with serrated edges, yellow capacitors and varistors black as tar,

                 shining and glossy as aquarium fish under living-room light,

And the miniature crystal towers of vacuum tubes,

       steel pins scaly as aged platinum,

Erector sets of gray plates and haloed getters intricate as space stations

       under sparkling glass.

In shapes like Coke bottles, potato mashers, and—my favorite—the tiny rockets

                 with arrowed heads

He called "Bugle Boys" for the labels of white-line cartoons,

       anthropomorphized tubes

       blowing trumpets stamped on each of their sides.

"They make electric sound come *sweet*," he said, "like no can b'lieve . . ."

He'd spend evenings in the garage, soldering circuitry and studying schematics—

Blue zigzags and squiggles on gray paper that folded like army maps—

       checking his work.

Once the speakers were set in their walnut cabinets

And the amp out of its gold-mesh cage,

He asked me to listen while he balanced the stereo channels—a marvel—

And swapped input tubes, pulling pairs from the sagging pocket
of his aloha shirt,
The glass of them making a gentle clatter like tea or *sake* cups
As they knocked softly together when he dipped and swirled his fingers in,
pulling them out like fancy fish from a bowl.

He couldn't hear.
Or, rather, he couldn't *quite* hear, losing it from a lifetime
of cumulative, small misfortunes:
A fever as a child in McCully, guns and cannons while away at war at seventeen,
The job holding down a jackhammer, the job under jet engines at Kane`ohe Marine Base.
I knew every reason, though he never gave one himself.

"Sit here," he'd say,
Pointing to the carpeted floor in front of the beige sofa we never used.
He'd throw me a *zabuton* to sit on, tell me to concentrate,
And I'd hear measure after measure of Big Band tunes filling the room
Like airy clouds of brass cotton lofting around the lamps, ashtrays,
and coconut curios around me.
"American Patrol," "Ciribiribin," and "Shake Down the Stars" took turns
With lush vibraphones and strummed `ukes—'50s hotel music from the Islands.

"Tell me whatchu hearing," he'd say, and I would, my father taking notes,
Smiling over our evenings of pleasurable work, string basses and horns in my ears,
Kick drums and toms reverberating through the floorboards,
Sinatra swaggering a tune, just behind the beat.

What did I know of travail or passion then? My father trying to beat the clock,
Hastening to hear or not hear each spinning A-side he ever danced to
at the Black Cat in Honolulu

Before the world closed its cave of cotton around him,

Cymbals become a silent splash of metallic light, snare rolls a strobe of sticks
        with no sound,

A song only a murmur without scale,

                    and music a birthplace he could never return to.

"No ka ipo lei . . . manu," sang the Sons of Hawai`i, and so I said they did,

My father jotting it down, Bugle Boys jousting in the pocket of his shirt.

Chikin Hekka

Thwock! Thwock! Thwock!
was the rhythmic chopping of steel on butcher block near the sink,
Kubota wielding the cleaver's long, narrow blade like it was a machete cutting cane,
Bringing it along the back and legs of the raw carcass in quick, pistonlike strikes.
He was making *hekka*—a whole chicken cooked with bamboo shoots
      sliced thin as *sashimi,*
Fresh carrots in diagonal slivers like orange doubloons, and half-circles
Of cut round onions that tessellated and turned clear in a bubbling pot.

He'd make a broth of bonito flakes and black *shōyu,*
Then grab all he'd cut the way I'd seen him handle octopus
      in tinned buckets near the sea,
Scooping them in the basket of his hands, tentacles drooping
      like roots from a purple screwpine tree,
And dropping them in a waiting pot. And if they cried, Kubota didn't care,
Wind furling the big trouser legs of his khaki pants. It was the ocean that gave off
A rattling sigh of small stones and regret. *I cooking,* he would say,
And not the pink bits of chicken flesh nor white flecks of bone that spattered his glasses
And spotted the newspapered backsplash along the sinks and carving table
Would stay him from the *karma* of his task.

                        Aroma of blood and marrow,
Bright cymbal of a steel pot's lid, dipper of *kiawe* and spoon from the horn of a goat,
He made his humble kitchen a spectacle of sights and smells—
Petite, green armies of chopped celery sliding off the cutting board.
He'd take a bundle of bean threads, dry as graveyard sand, white as ashes of incense,
Twisting it like a rag in his hands until the strands sheared from his quick torque.
Shirataki, he'd say, *waterfall we call long rice,* but unlike steamed rice,
It turned golden in the slick of the stew, fattened in flavors of blended fish and fowl.

Winters, when the Oregon rains can damp my soul, I try to make it this way still,

And take the Viking cleaver down from its place, a household god over the sink,

Holding it up to the light so I can see the sheen of its edge against the outer dark,

And I swing it so flesh and fat spatter me awake to all the heroic good of his will.

Holiday in Honolulu

after a photograph

Billie in a yellow bikini and without the gardenia in her hair,
But instead a dark hibiscus, plump as her curls.
Next to her, Armstrong in Bermudas and a flat English driver's cap,
The famous grin spreading wide as the beach behind them.
And Trummy Young, that marooned trombonist from Gibson's Bar,
Dressed in a hotel robe and swim trunks, flanks her other side.

She looks shy, perhaps off the drugs or only lightly dosed,
Not quite sad, as the sun makes a light gleam off their skins.
I'd never thought of them here, American jazz greats,
      cavorting on the beach,
The big pink hotel looming just off Armstrong's right shoulder,
Celebrities among the tourists, bringing their brand of music
To mix in among the `ukulele, steel guitars, and falsetto tenors
                  of the hotels.
But Pahinui must have, his singing a short breath
      behind the beat sometimes,
Playing that slappy catch-up, tailgating to the rhythm
Like Satchmo, who showed Holiday how to do the same,
All hip to the bluesy, hesitation style—a kind of tease.

And didn't Gabby sound like Charlie Christian sometimes,
Strumming that guitar to a hula measure,
A half-beat off the One and swinging the pace
So the music had that feel of a five o'clock jump?

I don't know for sure, but musicologists tell me
Hawai`i was forever a crossroads, seaborne chants
From Polynesia circulating up via Tahitian canoe
And bouncing back from Rapa Nui,
Where only the *moai* survive now.
And then the missionary hymns crept in,

The falsetto yodel of Argentine *vaqueros*.
After that, Mississippi and Louisiana delta blues,
Swamp songs from the steamships through the Panama Canal,
Their deckhands exchanging licks with the local guitar-pickers,
Bottlenecks sliding like spit on Hotel Street.
Pretty soon, a *paniolo* puts the dull edge of his knife
On the open-tuned strings of a Dobro, and we get the lap-steel
And *hapa-haole* songs of mixed Hawaiian and English,
Chang-a-lang from the Portuguese, *kachi-kachi*
And *son montuno* from Puerto Rican cane and pineapple workers.

What's "original" anyway? *Indigenous* and *essentially* anything?

I'll take Holiday in Honolulu, plucking a red hibiscus
From a green hotel bush as she saunters from the lobby
Across the breezy *lanai* with the *tiki* torches aflame and smoking,
The scent of ginger flowers from `awapuhi* hotel soap on her skin,
Cocking her head to one side and pulling back the lush hair,
Placing the stem and pea-green corolla back behind an unjeweled ear,
Giving Armstrong and Trummy Young that bluesy wink of hers
As she adjusts the small bell of the bloom so it opens
Like a pliant, red trumpet in the sweetened airs of Waikīkī.

55

I'd thought my life too unfocused and without cause compared to Kubota's,
Myself too pampered and leisurely compared to my father, who worked until he dropped,
Dragon from the sky, laid out like he was asleep in the ER where he died,
Heart stopped mid-sentence speaking to the Filipino nurse at Gardena Memorial,
Catty-corner and not a block from where hustlers took up their spots
                                        at the velvet, five-draw tables.

But now, fifty-five today, I don't think I've wandered enough,
                                have had too much cause, if anything,
And need, in fact, a fuller sail of emptiness than I've allowed myself,
                                        spinning stars to steer by.
I need to let go, drift in the eddies as they swirl, meander as Wang Wei did,
                                        floating like a leaf
On one of his rivers, flowing through sun and shadows in the long swale of a garden.

I liked the terraces at Bellagio, for instance, the lavender grasses and rock walls,
Gravel and stone paths, wisteria hanging like grapes from the trellises,
The view of the lake from Pliny's promontory, full of solace and solitude.
I'd stroll out from my study and Montgomery, the Petrarch scholar,
Would be there sketching a charcoal of the olive grove filling in the infield
Of an S-curve on the approach road to the Villa below.
We'd invoke the pastoral, the bucolic idea the Classical ancients had
One could reattach the fecklessly civilized soul back to ground in Nature
By writing of shepherds and maids, goats and flowers . . .
"Or farmers and chickenshit," he said, turning from his work and grinning,
The white hair on his temples stark against the azure backdrop of the lake,
Froth of fragile, tendrilous waves like barber trimmings fallen from his head.

Or the shore of sand dunes, *wiliwili*, and sea grapes near the piggery in Kahuku.
Wind comes one way—stench of rotting kelp and fresh spume
                                from the barnacled and cowried sea.

Wind another way—and the scent of a mellow ordure might drive your pace faster
To the view of wetlands up the coast past the Marconi Station and shrimp ponds,
While the gulls peep and screech overhead, gust-jockeying and wind-roving
Like loose kites with no *karma* tying them down.

                                I'd like to do that—
Cut crosswind and sail thirty yards into forever, the earthly and human-bound
Irrelevant as an eyeball gazing upwards at my outline, V-wing
                                         on the Emersonian Transcendental,
Past without blemish, see-sawing heart without hesitation or pain.

A Map of Kahuku in Oregon

Far away from its sand dunes and perched beaches,
Its three landing strips for fighters and B-17s, circa 1941,
Far from the Marconi Station that failed to radio in the first wave—
Mitsubishi Zekes and Nakajima torpedo Kates on their flight to Pearl—
And far from the ponds and cemeteries that taught me sport and piousness,
I tape a map of it to the wall of my study—
The high-wave line, coastal slope and marshlands, its bays and points—
And look out my window to early spring in Oregon.
There's a slanting white gladness out there today,
Snow falling sideways and spinning around like dervishes.
I look at the plum trees in the side yard, expecting popcorn blooms,
But instead I see that a sheet of coral has laid itself on their boughs
And encircled our backyard with a thin, white reef.
At six months old, it's Annalena's first snow,
And I take her out on the deck. She blinks as the flakes
Fall on her face and on her lashes, making small crusts
Like a white mascara that melts invisible in an instant.
I'm a long way from what I know best, it seems,
Miserere from the Tallis Scholars on the stereo inside
Carrying out through the opened kitchen door,
Holy voices of English choristers filling what's missing,
Peace like a long reward after three generations of digging in,
Making a place on earth where the heart can be empty at last.
Who am I to come after such people who cut the cane
Along the narrow plantation acreages along the North Shore?
I've been told so many bits and pieces of story,
They don't add up—beachside graveyards being eaten by the sea
Where the Green Lady swirls like kelp in the tide surge,
The gold coins rummaged from a locked tool chest in the junkyard,
All overgrown with spinach and calabash until children,
Playing war games, pried it open and found them,
Undulled by time and shiny as the day they were stamped.

Someone would start a tale on the porch, another would sing,
Falsettos and parakeets flying through the shotgun house,
While petals of plumeria littered the lawn outside,
And mynah birds hopped and squawked by the hot road.
My sense of heaven was built like this, remembrance
Its gateless gate, the innocence of my child my inquisitor,
White algae of snow falling on every limb in the yard.

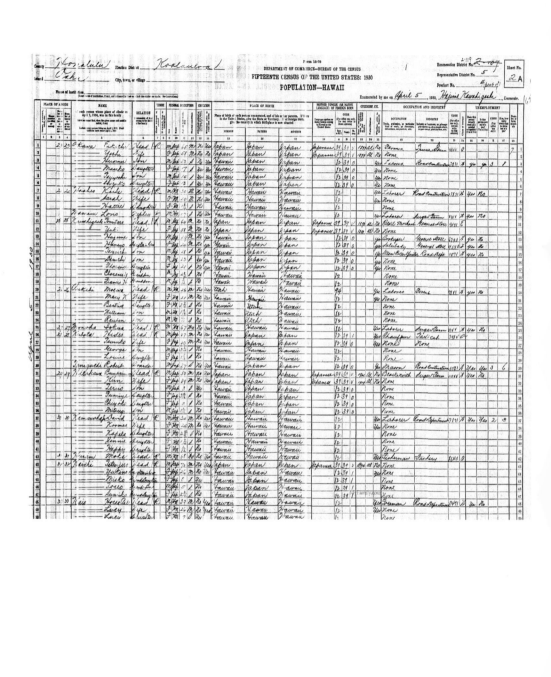

V

ELEGY

Elegy, Kahuku

To the memory of Herbert Shigemitsu, 1943–2004

A jut of sand and grass, the northern tip of O`ahu,

The family graves of two generations,

Is where I go on pilgrimage—

Scores of unmarked plots under temple grass,

Stakes of rotting 2x4s silvering through the processionals of rain,

Slanting like monks in gray robes

Bending to kneel in homage to the brutal earth.

There were cane fields all through this world once,

A sea of soft green between the emerald cliffs,

The folded rock screens of the Ko`olau

And pitching gray seas of the Pacific.

Rough lands made rougher by profit and calculation,

Whole villages imported to work the cane,

Nineteen cents a day for a man, eleven for women,

Bango tags stamped on their lunch pails

Half-full of rice and stringy beef,

Their bodies swaddled in denim against the cane dust,

Sweet muck of raw capital caked on their gloved hands.

Hore hore bushi, they sang, work tunes about "the man,"

A Scotch-Irish foreman with a whip and a pistol,

Or a Japanese with English skills sitting on a mule,

Counting the bob-and-weave of each brown soul

Hauling its bundle of burned stalks up the ramp of the cane car,

Chanting, bearing witness, testifying to the accomplishments of misery.

Gaman, they would say, "persevere,"

And *kodomo no tame,* "for posterity's sake,"

Grunting their way through resentment over the memory

Of handbills passed around the villages in southern Japan,
Promising "Heaven" in these islands,
Hawai`i as *tengoku* of the mid-Pacific.

And so they came, 188 in the first ship,
Swiftly 10,000 more, then more than that,
And my ancestors from Fukuoka, the Shigemitsu, immigrated too,
In the second wave of laborers under contract—
Kanyaku Imin, had their picture taken
Soon as they landed in Honolulu Bay
By a white man with an 8x10 who posed them on the docks.
In the photo, Katsutaro, my great-grandfather, sits cross-legged,
Dressed in a rough, dark cloth *kimono,*
Clutching my eldest granduncle who squirms in his grasp,
A child with his head shaven almost bald and a mole on his right cheek.
Katsutaro gazes straight into the camera with a look like Guevara's
As his head was lifted from the Bolivian autopsy table—astonished.
Mid-twenties I would guess, his stiff, bristling hair
Is cut close against his oblong head in an Ur-, nineteenth-century "fade."
Then, the amazing cultural touch of placing a *shamisen,*
That Japanese banjo, in Babasan's lap,
My great-grandmother off to his right.
She kneels and leans slightly into him,
Her dark face turned three-quarters from the lens,
Her eyes catching the tropical light,
Some bemusement curving her lips into a smile.
U-soh—"Bullshit is all," she might have thought,
This orchestrated pose of the dandy who met them at the Honolulu Bridge,
Offering them a few coins, then made the exposure for this amazing photograph.

*

It's in the Smithsonian now, third item in the "A More Perfect Union" exhibit,

Its entryway just to starboard of *Old Ironsides,* part of nation-making too.

Its provenance is through Tsuruko, my grandmother, who got it from Babasan,

Then gave it to Franklin Odo, a scholar who collects these things,

Who gave it to the Bishop Museum, who loaned it to the Smithsonian indefinitely.

I saw it first in a family album my grandmother pulled from under her bed

One hot afternoon in Nu`uanu, TV on to a Japanese game show,

Electric fan rattling and ringing in its cage, a mound of *somen* draining in the sink.

———

It's a long way from there to 1885, even longer to D.C. and the History Museum.

Yet provenance is not fate, the Shigemitsu and their seven children

Fleeing in the night, *michiyuki,* led by the moon across O`ahu's North Shore,

Evicted from their hut on Waialua Plantation in 1920 during a sugar strike

for better wages.

Tsuruko says they traipsed along the railroad tracks, hiding from *lunas,*

Stopping at fishing shrines and *lele*s at sunset

To cook rice and corned beef in a bucket, sleeping on beach sand and pine needles

Until they got to Kahuku and the haven of relatives

Who patched their clothes and salved their feet

And buried the youngest brother in the sandy point of the graveyard

Where most of them are now,

Laid to rest in the shadow of the smokestacks of the abandoned mill.

———

Once established in Kahuku, Babasan became known

For care and success with children, "because mos' of dem survive," Tsuruko said.

She was told to go along the dirt road through Walkerville

Where the whites all lived in their two-story houses

And out almost all the way to the piggery
To the stand of ironwood trees by the red fence at the dump.
Babasan went, and a woman met her there at midnight
With a newborn wrapped in a flannel shirt. Matsuo, they called him,
"Pine Boy," a Native Hawaiian adopted by the family,
Who grew to over six feet and worked and cursed the cane with his Japanese brothers.

————

To get there, you get off Kam Highway and go north through the village
Past the stacks of the rusting mill and along a crumbling paved road
Lined with morning glories and bougainvillea,
Until you get to the nine-hole public course built right against the sea.
My Uncle Harry was once its groundskeeper, a man barely five and a half feet tall,
Who could hit a mile with a 7-iron and drop a cruising seagull
With a shot from a sand wedge.

                    You park at the clubhouse,
Just a shack on stilts by the first hole and the Filipino graveyard,
And feel the trade winds billowing your loose clothes.
You bow and step through the horse gate and go down a grade
Past hole no. 5 and a bunker fringed with sea grapes growing out of the sand,
A screwpine twisting up the windblown trunk of a *hau* tree,
Sea-surf cannonades sending spume and spray on the soft kisses of wind.

I've taken my sons there a few times now,
Taught them the bows and genuflections of worship,
The murmurs of a chant, homage to the Other Side
I brought back with me from Shōkoku-ji in Kyoto.

They seem to like it when I bow, clap hands and sing,
And louder sing than the wind, knees plunged in the pokey grasses and sands of eternity.

I placed a cup of rice wine and a plate of *pake* cake on the grave,
Strung a wreath of purple orchids on the worn headstone of Yaeko Kubota,
My grandfather's sister, the last time we were there.

                                        I chanted the Heart Sutra,
"Form Is Emptiness, Emptiness Is Form," my sons holding their breaths,
Their postures of reverence like egrets posing in silver ponds near the sea.

Who comes here now?

                        Not my Auntie Ritsu, in Washington State
After fifty years of running the Kahuku 76 on Kamehameha, finishing out her days
In a nursing home near where her daughter lives, a letter carrier in Vancouver.
Not Cousin Trish in West L.A. or my mother in Gardena by the card clubs.
Hardly anyone except the wind that mutters none of our names,
Except waves from the sea that pound the breast of the earth.
Gulls cry and pipers scumble at the running tide on the sands of the point
Scrubbed clean of ash from the dead, traces of grief from the living
Drenched in blackened windrows ribboning against the last gold light.

———————

It is said they worshipped in the cane fields at first, chanted sutras by starlight,
Struck wooden bells the priests brought over from Hiroshima and Kumamoto.
They built the temple later, on the flat parade grounds across from the union hall.
Nothing's left now but a chorus of stars that sing in the abandoned cane at night

And whatever it is that makes me go back under it, fables I half-hear,
Recoveries from a childhood sitting on the floor around the Formica table
In the kitchen where the grown-ups talk-story of times past on holidays.

"There was a *benshi* once," a story begins, and its end is in whispers,
Love-making in the cane, chants of silk wrapped like silver on celluloid,
Illicit meetings of a wife and a storekeeper, *shinjū* in the sugar fields,
White chrysanthemums and broken bits of blue glass scattered with cremains on the sea.

———————

When *we* die, Kahuku is where we still go, no matter if the body is laid under palms
And a russet sky at Angelus-Rosedale on West Washington in Central L.A.
When my cousin Herbert died at sixty this year,
His brother Neal, at the funeral, giving the eulogy,
Spoke of our time as children gamboling amidst the cane,
Sword fights with cane tassels, screaming "I am the Count of Monte Kahuku!"
As we pursued joy through the neighborly stones of the graveyard,
Lifting piglets from the stalls of the piggery
As if they were our own desperate children rescued from the sea.

Will I go too?
                    Amidst the black, spiny urchins in tinned buckets
My grandfather has gathered from the crannies and stones of the outer reef?
In the slips of wind between ironwood and eucalyptus
        where Pine Boy became our foundling?
Tengoku it was called once, "The Domain of Heaven,"
And so it is whenever I say it is, sorrow like the silvered edge of a cloud,
Unmoored from *karma,* drifting on from memory to magnificence.

Notes

"An Oral History of Blind-Boy Liliko`i" is for Shuzo Uemoto.
"Hilo March" is by Joseph Kapaeau Ae`a, recorded by Sol Ho`opi`i and Louis Armstrong, among others.

"The Festival of San Giovanni" is for Shelly Withrow.

"Coral Road" is for the Shigemitsu Family Reunion, July 2004.

"Pupukea Shell" is for Wakako Yamauchi.
La bohème, by Giacamo Puccini, Luigi Illica, and Giuseppe Giacosa.

"A Child's Ark" is for Warren Nishimoto and Michi Kodama.

"The Wartime Letters of Hideo Kubota." During World War II, nearly five thousand Japanese Americans were held in eight detention camps run by the Department of Justice in Texas, Idaho, North Dakota, New Mexico, Arizona, and Montana. These detention facilities were separate from the internment camps run by the War Relocation Authority; held Buddhist ministers, Japanese language instructors, newspaper workers, and other community leaders; and were guarded by Border Patrol agents and U.S. military personnel. Many were not released until after the end of World War II. An abandoned Bureau of Indian Affairs boarding school in Leupp, Arizona, on the Navajo Indian Reservation, served as the Leupp Citizen Isolation Center for those considered problem inmates.

"Kubota to Miguel Hernández in Heaven, Leupp, Arizona, 1942" refers to "Lullaby to an Onion," by the Spanish Civil War poet who died in a fascist prison in 1942.

"Kubota to Nâzim Hikmet in Peredelkino, Moscow, from Leupp, Arizona" refers to several poems by the Turkish poet from *Things I Didn't Know I Loved,* translated by Mutlu Konoch and Randy Blasing (Persea, 1976).

"Kubota Writes to José Arcadio Buendía" addresses the character from *One Hundred Years of Solitude* by Gabriel García Márquez, translated by Gregory Rabassa (Harper and Row, 1970).

"Kubota to the Chinese Poets Detained on Angel Island." *Island: Poetry and History of Chinese Immigrants on Angel Island, 1910–1940,* edited and translated by Him Mark Lai, Genny Lim, and Judy Yung (University of Washington Press, June 1991).

"Kubota Returns to the Middle of Life" addresses the Polish poet Tadeusz Różewicz, who wrote "In the Middle of Life," translated by Czesław Miłosz in *Postwar Polish Poetry* (Penguin, 1970).

"Kubota Meets Pablo Neruda on the Street" borrows from "A Man Meets a Woman in the Street" by Randall Jarrell and samples from *The Heights of Macchu Picchu* by Pablo Neruda, translated by Nathaniel Tarn (Farrar, Straus and Giroux, 1967); from "Leaning into the Afternoons," translated by W. S. Merwin, *Twenty Love Poems and a Song of Despair* (Jonathan Cape, 1975); and from "Nothing but Death," translated by Robert Bly, *Neruda and Vallejo: Selected Poems* (Beacon Press, 1971).

"Kubota on Kahuku Point to Maximus in Gloucester" addresses Charles Olson, poet of Gloucester, Massachusetts, especially in his poem "Maximus, to himself" from *The Maximus Poems* (Jargon/Corinth, 1960) and in two documentary films in a series called *USA: Poetry* made by Richard O. Moore for WNET in 1965 and 1966.

"The Art of Fresco" is for Charles Wright, *maestro dell'universo misterioso.*

1. *The Expulsion from the Garden of Eden* by Masaccio, Cappella Brancacci, Florence. President William McKinley High School, Honolulu's first public high school, was known as "Tokio High" because so many Japanese Americans attended.

2. *Annalena Altarpiece* by Beato Angelico, Museo di San Marco, Florence.

3. "Gioto" in *Lives of the Painters,* Vasari.

4. *Noli me tangere,* by Beato Angelico, Convento di San Marco, Florence.

5. *The Prajnaparamita* (Heart Sutra), translated by Edward Conze in *Buddhist Scriptures* (Penguin Classics, 1959).

6. The Pablo O'Higgins murals at the ILWU Hall in Honolulu and a painting of Japanese laborers in Sprekelsville, Maui, by Joseph Dwight Strong, Jr. (1854–1899), 1885.

7. "Baptism" refers to the fresco *St. Peter Baptizing the Neophytes* by Masaccio, Cappella Brancacci, Florence.

9. "Roofscape" refers to the Duomo designed by Brunelleschi, Florence.

14. *"Yeux Glauques"* is taken from a poem of that name in *Hugh Selwyn Mauberly* by Ezra Pound.

15. "Soul's Leap" derives, in part, from a reading of "Directive" by Robert Frost and lines from Rodolfo's "Che gelida manina . . ." in Puccini's *La bohème.*

"Kawela Studies" is for Edward Hirsch.

"Bugle Boys." The Black Cat was a dance club in Honolulu, Hawai`i, circa World War II. *No ka ipo lei manu* means "For my cherished heart" and is a line in the lament "Ipo Lei Manu," written by Kapi`olani for Kalakaua in 1891.

"Holiday in Honolulu." Billie Holiday, Louis Armstrong, and Trummy Young on Waikīkī beach in front of the Royal Hawaiian Hotel. Photograph in the Bishop Museum Archives. Charles Philip "Gabby" Pahinui (1921–1980) was the great Hawaiian singer and slack-key guitarist who once said he'd learned his strumming style partly from listening to Django Reinhardt's Hot Club de France records.

"55." Ralph Waldo Emerson, "Nature."

"A Map of Kahuku in Oregon" is for Annalena LilySue Tsuruko Hongo.
Miserere is "Miserere mei, Deus" ("Have mercy on me, O God") by Gregorio Allegri and is a setting of Psalm 51. The line "Wash me, and I shall be whiter than snow" is in one of its verses.

"Elegy, Kahuku." William Butler Yeats, "Sailing to Byzantium."

Acknowledgments

Many thanks to the editors of the magazines and anthologies where these poems, some in previous versions, first appeared.

Amerasia Journal: "Chikin Hekka."

American Poetry Review: "Coral Road" and "55."

Georgia Review: "The Art of Fresco," "Elegy, Kahuku," and "An Oral History of Blind-Boy Liliko`i."

Harvard Review: "Waimea-of-the-Dead."

Honolulu Weekly: "Holiday in Honolulu."

Kenyon Review: "Kubota to the Chinese Poets Detained on Angel Island," "Kubota to Nâzim Hikmet in Peredelkino, Moscow, from Leupp, Arizona," and "Kubota on Kahuku Point to Maximus in Gloucester."

Louisville Review: "A Map of Kahuku in Oregon."

Ploughshares: "Kawela Studies," "Cane Fire," and "A Child's Ark."

Poetry Northwest: "The Festival of San Giovanni."

6moons.com: "Bugle Boys."

Slate: "Pupukea Shell."

Virginia Quarterly Review: "Kubota Writes to José Arcadio Buendía," "Kubota to Miguel Hernández in Heaven, Leupp, Arizona, 1942," "Kubota Returns to the Middle of Life," and "Kubota Meets Pablo Neruda on the Street."

I also wish to thank those who first read these poems. Gerald Ackerman and George Gorse read "The Art of Fresco," corrected errors regarding painting, the Italian language, and the fresco process, and made other helpful suggestions. T. R. Hummer offered useful criticism, also for "The Art of Fresco." Marie Carvalho and Nalani McDougall helped me with the Hawaiian language and local references. Stanleigh H. Jones Jr., Lynne Miyake, and Franklin Odo assisted me with the Japanese, Gaetano Prampolini with the Italian. Edward Hirsch, Dave Smith, and Deborah Garrison read the entire manuscript in its original draft and gave invaluable criticism to help reshape it and find its better nature.

At a crucial moment, David Mura, Russell Tomlin, and Samuel H. Yamashita each encouraged me to engage the heart of this work. A Summer Research Fellowship from the University of Oregon sponsored me in discovering some of the available background to this book archived in special collections at Brigham Young University–Hawaii and the Bishop Museum in Honolulu. A Durfee Fellowship at Pitzer College and a Rockefeller Foundation residency at the Bellagio Study Center in Lake Como, Italy, gave me the necessary peace to begin writing this book.

And, to Shelly Withrow, *Un dì . . . E da quel dì tremante, into the everlasting . . .*

Garrett Hongo was born in Volcano, Hawai`i, and grew up in Los Angeles. He is the author of two previous collections of poetry, three anthologies, and *Volcano: A Memoir of Hawai`i*. His poems and essays have appeared in *The Georgia Review, The Kenyon Review, The New York Times, Los Angeles Times, The New Yorker, Ploughshares, The American Poetry Review, Amerasia Journal, Raritan,* and *Virginia Quarterly Review,* among others. He has been the recipient of several awards, including fellowships from the NEA, the Guggenheim Foundation, and the Rockefeller Foundation. He teaches at the University of Oregon, where he is Distinguished Professor of Arts and Sciences.

A NOTE ON THE TYPE

The text of this book was composed in Palatino, a typeface designed by the noted German typographer Hermann Zapf. Named after Giovanni Battista Palatino, a writing master of Renaissance Italy, Palatino was the first of Zapf's typefaces to be introduced in America. The first designs for the face were made in 1948, and the fonts for the complete face were issued between 1950 and 1952. Like all Zapf-designed typefaces, Palatino is beautifully balanced and exceedingly readable.

Composed by North Market Street Graphics
Lancaster, Pennsylvania

Printed and bound by Thomson-Shore
Dexter, Michigan